GESTA PILATI;

OR THE

REPORTS, LETTERS AND ACTS

OF

PONTIUS PILATE,

PROCURATOR OF JUDEA,

With an Account of his Life and Death:

BEING

A TRANSLATION AND COMPILATION OF ALL THE WRIT-
INGS ASCRIBED TO HIM, AS MADE TO TIBERIUS
CÆSAR, EMPEROR OF ROME, CONCERNING
THE LIFE OF JESUS, HIS TRIAL
AND CRUCIFIXION.

WITH AN

INTRODUCTION AND NOTES

By W. O. CLOUGH, B. A.

_____

INDIANAPOLIS:
ROBERT DOUGLASS.
1880.

TABLE OF CONTENTS.

PART II.

PUBLISHER'S PREFACE.

The publisher, in issuing the second edition of this work, first offered to the American public last year, takes pleasure in announcing that the book is, after rigid review, offered in full confidence, as free from those minor errors that inevitably creep into all first editions.

The value and deep interest that attach to the contents of this book make it alike entertaining to all readers, who take any concern in Sacred Literature; and the general reception it has met at such hands, without regard to denominational lines, manifests the fact of its general importance to all who claim an interest in its remarkable records.

'The notices that have followed its perusal from scholarly men, both in and out of the Church, and which have been its only advertisement, are alike gratifying to the editor and publisher, and are the best guaranty of its value.

ROBERT DOUGLASS.

PREFACE TO THE SECOND EDITION.

The cordial reception of the first edition of the "Reports, Letters and Acts of Pilate" at the hands of ministers of the gospel of all denominations, of many of our most gifted educators in colleges and seminaries, and by many intelligent readers both within and without the church, has induced the editor to put forth the work in its present form, and for the reasons following:

The time is already present when it must be shown that Jesus Christ is an historic person. The life of Jesus is the center of the religious controversies that agitate our age, and the great question that demands solution is whence is the man Jesus? Is he an historical person or is he not? The settlement of this one question, says the eminent Tischendorf, is decisive of the question whether the Church shall or shall not live—the most momentous of all questions which the Church has to encoun-

ter. To rob him of his historic greatness, and yet
to think to retain the Christian faith and the
Christian Church, is a futile attempt, a vain mock-
ery, says the same eminent critic and writer.

It becomes, therefore, the duty of all Christians,
and especially of our clergymen, theological students
and professors, to furnish themselves from the ar-
mory of history with the weapons that alone can
be employed in the overthrow of that unbelief up-
held by a well organized movement, which to-day
threatens to convert theological science into soph-
istry, and so give powerful support to the anti-
christian spirit of our time. To do this must be
done by rigid inquiry in the field of historic re-
search, rather than by any other direction or
through any other means. *Jesus* did not scruple to
stand before kings or governors, nor scribes or
doctors. His *apostles* did not fear to plead before
the elders, the priests, the kings, the governors nor
emperors. Their advocacy *was fearless because invulnerable* in its claims, whether in an humble
Jewish synagogue or in the halls of philosophy, at
Jerusalem or in Rome. They spoke well attested
facts; they bore incontestable testimony to those
facts, and this alone made them invincible and invulnerable.

Can we do the same to-day? Are *we* invincible

and invulnerable?—historically, I mean. Can we stand before such a tribunal as the Roman Senate and the Emperor, as stood Justin Martyr? Can we allege that the facts occurring in the presence of his own appointed governor, Pontius Pilate, and reported by him, were facts in his own possession, written in the official documents made under his governor's own knowledge, and claim that they were fulfilled in the person of Jesus Christ? If we can we ought *to do it*, and if we can not we ought to *know* the reason why, and to acknowledge our shame that it has been stated by Christian writers that it ever was done. Who are these Christian writers? No less men than our Justin Martyr, our Tertullian, and our father of history in the Church, Eusebius. When did they do these things or report that they were done? In the year A. D. 138, Justin; about the year A. D. 200, Tertullian, and about A. D. 315, Eusebius.

These are the men. They are prominent and widely, widely known. We have their writings. They were all scholars, learned men, cultured men, *eminent* for their learning. They knew of the reports which Pilate made from Judea to his emperor, Tiberius Cæsar, at Rome, concerning Jesus. They knew what they contained as to the wonderful occurrences at, before and after the crucifixion. They were not only acquainted with all this, but were bold (two of these at least, Justin and Tertullian) to tell the highest man in Rome that *he* did or could know these wonderful things about Jesus by simple reference to the papers drawn up under Pontius Pilate. This is simply the history in brief of the Pilate papers as known to these three eminent men, Justin, Tertullian and Eusebius. Every Christian ought to know such an important scrap of history, and, *if* possible, obtain the papers of Pilate, and to know that it is his duty to circulate such respectable testimony as they contain, as did the good and eminent men above named, bear it before the great Emperor and his Roman Senate and to the world around them.

The reader of these lines need not be in doubt as to the papers, or the testimony they bear, for the reason that he may fear that the papers have been lost or destroyed, as they were attempted to be in A. D. 311, under Maximin's reign. We adduce authority here which will allay any fear and cast out all doubt as to whether *we have* the Pilate papers. We adduce the remarks of Dr. Constantine Tischendorf as taken from Mr. William L. Gage's translation, under the sanction of Dr. Tischendorf, and as found in his "Origin of the Four Gospels."

(See Origin of the Four Gospels, by Constantine

Tischendorf, p. 141, et seq. American Tract Society, 28 Cornhill, Boston, 1868.)

We adduce him as the most competent and intelligent critic in the matter under question. In commenting upon these papers of Pilate's, Dr. Tischendorf says:

"Justin, in like manner as before, is the most ancient voucher for this work, which is said to have been written under Pilate's jurisdiction, and by reason of its specification of wonderful occurrences before, during and after the crucifixion, to have borne strong evidence to the divinity of Christ. Justin saw as little reason as Tertullian and others for believing that it was a work of pious deception from a Christian hand." [As has been alleged often by opponents.] "On the contrary, Justin appeals to it twice in his first apology in order to confirm the accounts of the occurrences which took place at the crucifixion in accordance with prophecy, and of the miraculous healings effected by Christ, also the subject of prophetic announcement. He cites specifically (chap. 35) from Isaiah LXV. 2, and LVIII. 2: 'I have spread out my hands all the day unto a rebellious people which walketh in a way that was not good. They ask of me the ordinances of justice; they take delight in approaching to God.' Further, from the 22d Psalm: 'They pierced my hands and my feet; they parted my garments upon them and cast lots upon my vesture.' With reference to this he remarks that Christ fulfilled this; that he did stretch forth his hands when the Jews crucified him—the men who contended against him and denied that he was Christ. 'Then,' he says further, 'as the prophet foretold, they dragged him to the judgment seat, set him upon it and said, 'judge us.' The expression, however, 'they pierced,' etc., refers to the nails with which they fastened his feet and hands to the cross. And after they had crucified him they threw lots for his clothing, and they who had taken part in the act of crucifixion divided it among themselves.' To this he adds: 'And you can learn from the Acts, composed during the governorship of Pontius Pilate, that these things really happened.'

"Still more explicit is the testimony of Tertullian. It may be found in Apologeticus (chap. 2), where he says that out of envy Jesus was surrendered to Pilate by the Jewish ceremonial lawyers, and by him, after he had yielded to the cries of the people, given over for crucifixion; that while hanging on the cross he gave up the ghost with a loud cry, and so anticipated the executioner's duty; that at that same hour the day was interrupted by a sudden darkness; that a guard of soldiers was set at the grave for the purpose of preventing his disciples stealing his body, since he had predicted his resurrection, but that on the third day the ground was suddenly shaken and the stone rolled away from before the sepulcher; that in the grave nothing was found but the articles used in his burial; that the report was spread abroad by those who stood outside that the disciples had taken the body away; that Jesus spent forty days with them in Galilee, teaching them what their mission should be, and that after giving them their instructions as to what they should preach, he was raised in a cloud to heaven. Tertullian closes this account with the words, 'All this was reported to the Emperor at that time, Tiberius, by Pilate, his conscience having compelled even him to become a Christian.'

"The document now in our possession corresponds with this evidence of Justin and Tertullian. Even in the title it agrees with the account of Justin, although instead of the word *acta* which he used, and which is manifestly much more Latin than Greek, a Greek expression is employed which can be shown to have been used to indicate genuine Acts. The details recounted by Justin and Tertullian are all found in our text of the Acts of Pilate, with this variation, that nothing corresponds to what is joined to the declaration of the prophet, 'They dragged him to the seat of judgment and set him upon it and said,' etc. Besides this, the casting lots for the vesture is expressed simply by the allusion to the division of the clothes. We must give even closer scrutiny to one point. Justin alludes to the miracles which were performed in fulfillment of Old Testament prophecy, on the lame, the dumb, the blind, the dead and on lepers. In fact, in our Acts of Pilate, there are made to appear before the Roman governor a palsied man who had suffered for thirty-eight years, and was brought in a bed by young men, and healed on the Sabbath day; a blind man cured by the laying on of hands; a cripple who had been restored; a leper who had been cleansed; the woman whose issue of blood had been stanched, and a witness of the raising of Lazarus from the dead. Of that which Tertullian cites we will adduce merely the passage found in no one of our gospels, that Jesus passed forty days after his resurrection in company with his disciples in Galilee.

"This is indicated in our Acts of Pilate at the end of the fifteenth chapter, where the risen man is represented as saying to Joseph: 'For forty days go not out of thy house, for behold I go to my brethren in Galilee.'

"Every one will perceive how strongly the argument that our Acts of Pilate are the same which Justin and Tertullian read is buttressed by these unexpected coincidences. The assertion recently made requires, consequently, no labored contradiction that the allusions to both men have grown out of their mere suspicion that there was such a record as the Acts of Pilate, or out of the circulation of a mere story about such a record, while the real work was written as the consequence of these allusions at the close of the third century. What an uncommon fancy it requires in the two men to coincide so perfectly in a single production, as is the case in the Acts to which I am now referring. And are we to imagine that they referred with such emphasis as they employed to the mere creations of their fancy?

"The question has been raised with more justice, whether the production in our possession may not have been a copy or a free revision of the old and primitive one. The modern change in the title has given support to this conjecture, for it has occasioned the work to be commonly spoken of as the Gospel of Nicodemus. But this title is borne neither by any Greek manuscript, the Coptic-Sahidian papyrus, nor the Latin manuscripts, with the exception of a few of the most recent. It may be traced only subsequently to the twelfth century, although at a very early period, in one of the two prefaces attached to the work, Nicodemus is mentioned in one place as a Hebrew author and in another as a Greek translator. But aside from the title, the hand-writing displays great variation, and the two prefaces alluded to above show clearly the work of two hands. Notwithstanding this, however, there are decisive grounds for holding that our Acts of Pilate contains in its main substance the document drawn from Justin and Tertullian. The first of this to be noticed is, that the Greek text, as given in the version most widely circulated in the manuscripts, is surprisingly corroborated by two documents of the rarest character, and first used by myself—a Coptic-Sahidian papyrus manuscript and a Latin palimpsest—both probably dating from the fifth century. Such a documentary confirmation of their text is possessed by scarcely ten works of the collective Greek classic literature. Both of these ancient writings make it in the highest degree probable that the Egyptian and Latin translations which they contain were executed still earlier.

"But could a work which was held in great consideration in Justin's and Tertullian's time and down to the commencement of the fourth century, and which strenuously insists that the Emperor

Maximin caused other blasphemous Acts of Pilate
to be published and zealously circulated, manifestly
for the purpose of displacing and discrediting the
older Christian Acts—could such a work suddenly
change its whole form, and from the fifth century,
to which in so extraordinary a manner translators,
wholly different in character, point back with such
wonderful concurrence, continue in the new form?
Contrary as this is to all historical criticism, there
is in the contents of the work, in the singular manner in which isolated and independent details are
shown to be related to the canonical books, no less
than in the accordance with the earliest quotations
found in Justin and Tertullian, a guaranty of the
greatest antiquity.

"There are in the contents, also, matters of such
a nature that we must confess that they are to be
traced back to the primitive edition, as, for exam-
ple, the narrative in the first chapter of the bringing forward of the accused.

"It is incorrect, moreover, to draw a conclusion
from Justin's designation of the Acta which is not
warranted by the whole character of the work.
The Acta, the ὑπομνήματα, are specified in Justin's
account, not less than in the manuscripts which we
possess, as being written *under* Pontius Pilate, and

2

that can signify nothing else than that they were
an official production composed under the direct
sanction of the Roman Governor."

Such are the statements of Tischendorf in regard
to the remarkable papers presented in the latter
portion of this volume. Whatever else he may
have said of them in relation to their connection
with our Scriptures, one thing he has most clearly
affirmed, viz., *that we are to-day in possession* of the
papers transmitted by Pilate to the Roman Emperor, as seen, known and read by Justin and Tertullian and others, and as alluded to by Eusebius.
The simple question remaining to be settled by the
reader is this: Are we to accept them as Justin,
Tertullian and Eusebius did, as the official statements of Pilate, originating in his procuratorship
in Judea and written under his knowledge and with
his sanction, or are we to assume as some have done,
that these three eminent men spoke and wrote of
matters of the highest importance to all coming
generations without a correct appreciation of what
they were doing? Such persons as are capable of
casting aside the plain and emphatic statements of
Justin Martyr, Tertullian and Eusebius made to the
Roman Senate, an educated Emperor, and to philosophers, from A. D. 138 down to A. D. 315 in regard to these papers of Pilate—genuine copies of

which we possess to-day, according to this re-
nowned scholar and critic, whose language has been
accurately quoted above—such persons, I say, are
prepared to cast aside the oldest and best apologists
for christianity, the ablest of church historians, and
the profoundest of modern historical critics in regard to the man Jesus and his history.

And I must not omit to remark that such persons are often met with, not knowing how illogical
it is to accept at the hands of a historian such portion of his testimony as suits our purpose in any
given case and to reject his testimony in cases of
much greater moment. Christian scholars and
critics make great use of Justin and Tertullian in
appeals to their writings in establishing the number, the age, and the contents of our gospels. They
always speak of the learned historian, Eusebius, as
the "father of Church history."

The whole world of enlightened scholarship refers to Tischendorf as an eminent scholar and critic
in biblical archæology. And these are the men
whom we have brought forward here, to show from
the first three, that the Pilate papers were in existence prior to A. D. 138; that they were accepted as
the well known history of the occurrences which
they detail, and that they were among the public
records of Roman officials even down to the begin-

ning of the fourth century, and from the last one of these to show that the papers mentioned by the first three are still in existence *and in our possession.* We have allowed each one of the four to speak in his own words, for himself, without presuming to put a syllable to or take from the words of such competent and eminent witnesses. We leave the impartial reader to judge whether the witnesses here adduced have made out the conclusion—that we are in possession of Pilate's records concerning Jesus Christ.

It is but just, however, to the reader of the foregoing criticisms of Dr. Tischendorf, to him and to all whose names occur in this discussion, to disclose here the theory of Dr. Tischendorf, and to discuss briefly the same for the benefit of such readers as may not have had opportunity of reading him at length. In the main body of his criticism on the Acts of Pilate, it is evident that he labors to show, does show the antiquity and genuineness of these papers. He, in plain words, says *we have the papers substantially,* read and used by Justin in A. D. 188. He leaves no doubt on this point whatever. He, moreover, as plainly states that these papers made *under* Pontius Pilate were in existence in Tertullian's time, and even down to the beginning of the fourth century, as Eusebius has

so fully told. The only difficulty that can possibly
arise in a clear and impartial mind in scanning Dr.
Tischendorf's whole criticism on these papers, is
this: It is intimated at the outset and affirmed at the
close, that a very singular relationship subsists between these papers and John's Gospel. In plain
words, that one is dependent on the other. Can this
affirmation be sustained without a most damaging
reflection upon Justin, Tertullian and Eusebius?
Imagine Justin before the Roman Senate, before
its Emperor, and before the learning of Rome's
acutest philosophers, affirming with emphasis, "*You
may know by, or from the papers drawn up under Pilate, that these things are so.*" Conceive of a more
ridiculous appeal in all history than was this of
Justin, if we are to rob him of his wits here. I say
it with severe emphasis: Justin Martyr could
never have done such an act as has been intimated
he did do, when he made his appeal to certain public records of Rome in confirmation of the truths
he uttered concerning the occurrences of the crucifixion of Jesus, and did not know that he was
appealing to records never in existence. It is un-
reasonable to suppose that such a man as Justin
would allege in the face of the very custodians of
these documents what he is reported to have alleged.
" Pilate, himself sent an account to Tiberius, then

emperor." This is the allegation of Tertullian, in substance the same as that of Justin; or to quote Dr. Tischendorf's own words in giving Justin's account, "written *under* Pontius Pilate." This is Justin's allegation as quoted from Tischendorf's own rendering. But how shall we get rid of Dr. Tischendorf's difficulty if we admit that Justin and Tertullian were correct in claiming the actual existence of papers really "sent by Pilate himself," "written under Pontius Pilate?" How shall we save Justin's and Tertullian's reputation as truthful and competent witnesses? By no means whatever, without severing the alleged relation between John's Gospel and the Acts of Pilate. And every clear and impartial thinker will perceive, I think, that it is far better to sever that relation, if without hurt either to John's Gospel or to the character of Justin, Tertullian and Eusebius, than allege its existence to the infinite wounding of these three men. And the theory of this relation between John's Gospel and the Acts of Pilate manifestly can not be sustained except by impugning the intelligence of Justin, Tertullian and Eusebius. It openly and plainly puts them to the hazzard of appealing to mere forgeries not possibly older than fifty years in Justin's time, and the very time of his appeal. Can it be possible that Justin appealed to

forgeries *not fifty* years old, and alleged them to be
accounts " written under Pontius Pilate," and this
in the face of the custodians of those very accounts? Is it not contrary to sound judgment, to
ordinary intelligence in him? Can we not affirm
the like of Tertullian, who substantially and more
distinctly has set forth what has here been related
by Justin? Clearly there is but one solution to this
difficulty, the abandonment of the theory of the
connection between John's Gospel and the Acts of
Pilate, and by affirming what is most probable in
the case, that although the same facts in similar
terms are expressed in both writings, it does not
necessarily follow that one is dependent on the
other. The Acts of Pilate must have been written
anterior to John's Gospel if "written under Pontius Pilate," and could not in that case depend
upon, allude to, or have any connection with John's
Gospel. That they were so written is affirmed by
Justin, Tertullian and Eusebius, three eminent
witnesses, who ought to have known whether these
accounts were "written under Pontius Pilate" or
whether they were compilations from writings made
fifty years after Pilate's departure from Judea;
compilations of men writing them three score years
and ten after the recall of Pilate from Judea to
Rome. It is almost certain they did know. To

charge that they did not, but were appealing to forgeries not fifty years old in Justin's day, and declaring the fabrications of their Christian brethren to be official records "written under Pilate and sent by him to Tiberius," is the only way by which the allegation of connection between the Acts of Pilate and John's Gospel can be sustained.

This, then, is a clear statement of the whole question in relation to the Acts of Pilate—as to antiquity and genuineness of the same in the copies we possess, and as to the relation alleged to subsist between these papers and John's Gospel. We leave to the reader and to the Christian world to say whether these testimonies to the divinity of Jesus, made to the highest court of the world by the best and most competent witnesses, in an age when all the events and occurrences were fresh in the minds of all, shall or shall not be thrown aside as a part of the history of the life of Jesus—with one single remark only—that is: these testimonies are of the same quality identically as those upon which we must rely and have always relied for determining historically the genuineness of our Four Gospels. And if the testimony has been substantiated, it is more valuable than any and all other that has come to us from writings outside the Gospels themselves.   W. O. C.

SKETCH OF THE LIFE OF PONTIUS PILATE.

The prænomen of Pontius Pilate is unknown. The name indicates that he was connected, by decent or adoption, with the gens Pontii, first conspicuous in Roman history in the person of C. Pontius Telesinus, the great Samnite general. The cognomen Pilatus has received two explanations: (1.) As armed with the pilum or javelin; compare "pilata agmina." [Virgil's Eneid, xii. 121.] (2.) As contracted from pileatus. The fact that the pileus or cap was the badge of manumitted slaves, makes it probable that the epithet marked him out as a *libertus* or the descendant of one. Of the early history of Pilate we know nothing; but a German legend fills up the gap strangely enough. Pilate is the bastard son of Tyrus, King of Mayence. His father sends him to Rome as a hostage. There he is guilty of a murder; but being sent to Pontus, rises into notice as subduing the barbarous tribes

(25)

there, receives in consequence the name of Pontius
and is sent to Judea. It has been thought that
the twenty-second legion, which was in Palestine
at the time of the destruction of Jerusalem and was
afterwards stationed at Mayence, may have been
in this case the bearer of this tradition.

Pontius Pilate was the sixth Roman procurator
of Judea, and under him our Lord worked, suffered and died, as we learn, not only from the
obvious Scripture allusions, but from Tacitus. A
procurator was generally a Roman knight, appointed to act under a governor of a province as
collector of the revenue and judge in cases connected with it.

Strictly speaking, procurators of Cæsar were only
required in the imperial provinces; that is, in those
which, according to the constitution of Augustus,
were reserved for the especial administration of
the emperor, without the intervention of the Senate and people, and governed by his legate. In
the senatorian provinces, governed by proconsuls,
the corresponding duties were discharged by quæs-
tors. Yet, it appears, that sometimes procurators
were appointed in these provinces also to collect
certain dues of the *fiscus* (the emperor's special
revenue) as distinguished from those of the *ærarium*
(the revenue administered by the Senate). Some-

times in a small territory, especially in one con-
tiguous to a larger province, and dependent upon it,
the procurator was head of the administration and
had military and judicial authority, though he was
responsible to the governor of the neighboring
province. Thus, Judea was attached to Syria upon
the deposition of Archelaus, A. D. 6, and a procurator appointed to govern it, with Cæsarea for its
capital. Already, during a temporary absence of
Archelaus, it had been in charge of the procurator
Sabinus; then, after that ethnarch's banishment,
came Coponius; the third procurator was M. Am-
bivus; the fourth, Annius Rufus; the fifth, Valerius Gratus; and the sixth, Pontius Pilatus, who
was appointed A. D. 25–26, in the twelfth year of
Tiberius. One of his first acts was to remove the
headquarters of the army from Cæsarea to Jerusalem. The soldiers, of course, took with them their
standards bearing the image of the emperor, into
the holy city. No previous governor had ventured
on such an outrage. Pilate had been obliged to
send them in the night, and there were no bounds,
to the rage of the people, in discovering what had
been thus done. They poured down in crowds
upon Cæsarea, where the procurator was residing,
and besought him to remove the images. After
five days of discussion he gave the signal to some

concealed soldiers to surround the petitioners and put them to death, unless they ceased to trouble him; but this only strengthened their determination, and they declared themselves ready rather to die than forego their resistance to an idolatrous innovation.

Pilate then yielded, and the standards were then, by his orders, brought down to Cæsarea. On two other occasions he nearly drove the Jews to insurrection; the first, when in spite of this warning about the images, he hung up in his palace at Jerusalem some gilt shields inscribed with the names of deities, which were only removed by an order from Tiberius; the second, when he appropriated the revenue arising from the redemption of vows to the construction of an aqueduct. This order led to a riot, which he suppressed by sending among the crowd soldiers, with concealed daggers, who massacred a great number, not only rioters, but of casual spectators. To these specimens of his administration, which rest on the testimony of profane authors, we must add the slaughter of certain Galileans, which was told to our Lord as a piece of news, and on which he founded some remarks on the connection between sin and calamity. It must have occurred at some feast at Jerusalem in the outer court of the Temple, since the blood of the

worshipers was mingled with their sacrifices; but
the silence of Josephus about it seems to show that
riots and massacres, on such occasions, were so
frequent that it was needless to recount them at all.

It was the custom of the procurators to reside at
Jerusalem during the great feasts, to preserve order;
and, accordingly, at the time of our Lord's last
passover, Pilate was occupying his official residence
in Herod's palace; and to the gates of this palace,
therefore, Jesus, condemned on the charge of blasphemy, was brought early in the morning by the
chief priests and officers of the Sanhedrim, who
were unable to enter the residence of a Gentile,
lest they should be defiled and unfit to eat the
passover. Pilate, therefore, came out to learn their
purpose and demanded the nature of the charge.
At first they seem to have expected that he would
carry out their wishes without further inquiry;
and, therefore, merely described our Lord as a disturber of the peace; but as a Roman procurator
had too much respect for justice, or at least under-
stood his business too well to consent to such a
condemnation, and as they knew he would not enter
into theological questions any more than Gallio
did on a somewhat similar occasion, they were
obliged to devise a new charge, and, therefore, interpreted our Lord's claims in a political sense,

accusing him of assuming the royal title, perverting the nation, and forbidding the paying of tribute to Rome.

It is plain, that from this moment Pilate was distracted between the two conflicting feelings; a fear of offending the Jews, who had already grounds of accusation against him, which would be strengthened by any show of lukewarmness in punishing an offense against the imperial government, and a conscious conviction that Jesus was innocent, since it was absurd to suppose that a desire to free the nation from Roman authority was criminal in the eyes of the Sanhedrim. Moreover, this latter feeling was strengthened by his own hatred of the Jews, whose religious scruples had caused him frequent trouble, and by a growing respect for the calm dignity and meekness of the sufferer. First, he examined our Lord privately, and asked him whether he was a king? The question which he, in turn, put to his judge, "Sayest thou this of thyself, or did others tell it thee of me?" seems to signify that there was, in Pilate's own mind, a suspicion that the prisoner really was not what he was charged with being; a suspicion which shows itself in a later question, "Whence art thou?" in the increasing desire to release him, and in the refusal to alter the inscription on the cross. In any case Pilate accepted, as satisfactory, Christ's assurance that his *kingdom* was not of this world, that is, not worldly in its nature or objects, and therefore, not to be founded by this world's weapons, though he could not understand the assertion that it was to be established by bearing witness to the truth. His famous reply, " What is truth?" was the question of a worldly-minded politician; skeptical, because he was indifferent; one who thought truth an empty name, or at least could not see " any connection between truth and policy." With this question he brought the interview to a close, and came out to the Jews and declared the prisoner innocent. To this they replied that his teaching had stirred up all the people from Galilee to Jerusalem. The mention of Galilee suggested to Pilate a new way of escaping from his dilemma, by sending on the case to Herod Antipas, tetrarch of that country, who had come up to Jerusalem to the feast, while at the same time it gave him an opportunity of making overtures of reconciliation to Herod, with whose jurisdiction he had probably in some recent instance interfered. But Herod, though propitiated by this act of courtesy, declined to enter into the matter, and merely sent Jesus back to Pilate dressed in shining, kingly robes, to express his ridicule of such pretensions, and contempt for the whole business. So Pilate was compelled to come to a decision, and, first having assembled the chief priests and also the people, whom he probably summoned in the expectation that they would be favorable to Jesus, he announced to them all that the accused had done nothing worthy of death, but at the same time in hopes of pacifying the Sanhedrim, he proposed to scourge him before he released him. But as the accusers were resolved to have his blood, they rejected this concession, and, therefore, Pilate had recourse to a fresh expedient. It was the custom for the Roman governor to grant every year, in honor of the Passover, pardon to one condemned criminal. The origin of the practice is unknown, though we may mention it with the fact mentioned by Livy that at a Lectisternium "vinctis quoque dempta vincula."

Pilate, therefore, offered the people their choice between two, the murderer Barabbas and the prophet, whom a few days before they had hailed as the Messiah. To receive their decision, he ascended the bema, a portable tribunal which was carried about with a Roman magistrate, to be placed wherever he might direct, and which in the present instance was erected on a tessellated pavement in front of the palace, and called in Hebrew Gab-

batha, probably from being laid down on a slight
elevation. As soon as Pilate had taken his seat,
he received a mysterious message from his wife—
according to tradition, a proselyte of the gate,
named Procla, or Procula, "who had suffered many
things in a dream," which impelled her to entreat
her husband not to condemn the Just One. But
he had no longer any choice in the matter, for the
rabble, instigated of course by the priests, chose
Barabbas for pardon, and clamored for the death of
Jesus; insurrection seemed imminent, and Pilate
reluctantly yielded. But before issuing the fatal
order, Pilate washed his hands before the multitude
as a sign that he was innocent of the crime, in
imitation, probably, of the ceremony enjoined in
Deut. xxi., where it is ordered that when the per-
petrator of a murder is not discovered, the elders
of the city in which it occurs shall wash their
hands, with the declaration, " Our hands have not
shed this blood, neither have our eyes seen it."

Such a practice might be adopted even by a
Roman, as intelligible to the Jewish multitude
around him. As in the present case it produced
no effect, Pilate ordered his soldiers to inflict the
scourging preparatory to execution; but the sight
of unjust suffering so patiently borne, seems again

3

to have troubled his conscience and prompted a new effort in favor of the victim. He brought him out bleeding from the savage punishment, and decked in the scarlet robe and crown of thorns, which the soldiers had put on him in derision, and said to the people, "Behold the man!" hoping that such a spectacle would rouse them to shame and compassion. But the priests only renewed their clamors for his death, and fearing that the political charge of treason might be insufficient, returned to their first accusation of blasphemy, and, quoting the law of Moses, which punished blasphemy with stoning, declared that he must die, " because he made himself the Son of God." But this title, Son of God, augmented Pilate's superstitious fears, already aroused by his wife's dream; he feared that Jesus might be one of the heroes or demigods of his own mythology; he took him again to the palace, and inquired anxiously into his descent and his claims, and as the question was prompted by fear or curiosity, Jesus made no reply. When Pilate reminded him of his own absolute power over him, he closed this last conversation with the irresolute governor by the mournful remark, "Thou couldst have no power at all against me, except it were given from above; therefore, he that delivered me unto these hath the greater sin."

God had given to Pilate power over him, and
power only; but to those ¡who delivered him up
God had given the means of judging of his claims;
and, therefore, Pilate's sin in merely exercising his
power was less than theirs, who, being God's own
priests, with the Scriptures before them, and the
word of prophecy still alive among them, had de-
liberately conspired for his death. The result of
this interview was one last effort to save Jesus by
a fresh appeal to save the multitude; but now arose
the formidable cry, "If thou let this man go, thou
art not Cæsar's friend," and Pilate, to whom political success was as the breath of life, again ascended
the tribunal, and finally pronounced the desired
condemnation. So ended Pilate's share in the
greatest crime which has been committed since the
world began. That he did not immediately lose
his feelings of anger against the Jews, who had
thus compelled his acquiescence, and of compassion
and awe for the sufferer, whom he had un-
righteously sentenced, is plain from his curt and
angry refusal to alter the inscription which he had
prepared for the cross, his ready acquiescence in
the request made by Joseph of Arimathæa that the
Lord's body might be given up to him rather than
consigned to the common sepulchre reserved for
those who had suffered capital punishment, and

his sullen answer to the demand of the Sanhedrim that the sepulchre should be guarded. So far as Scripture is concerned, our knowledge of Pilate ends here. But we learn from Josephus that his anxiety to avoid giving offense to Cæsar did not save him from political disaster. The Samaritans were unquiet and rebellious. A leader of their own race had promised to disclose to them the sacred treasures which Moses was reported to have concealed in Mount Gerizim. Pilate led his troops against them, and defeated them easily enough.

The Samaritans complained to Vitellius, now president of Syria, and he sent Pilate to Rome to answer their accusations before the emperor. When he reached Rome he found Tiberius dead, and Caius (Caligula) on the throne, A. D. 36. Eusebius adds that soon afterwards, "wearied with misfortunes," he killed himself. As to the scene of his death there are various traditions. One is that he was banished to Vienna Allobrogum, where a singular monument, a pyramid on a quadrangular base 52 feet high, is called Pontius Pilate's tomb. Another is that he sought to hide his sorrow on the mountain by the lake of Lucerne, now called Mount Pilatus; and there, after spending years in its recesses, in remorse and despair rather than penitence, plunged into the dismal lake which occupies its summit.

The character of Pilate may be sufficiently inferred from the foregoing sketch of his conduct at our Lord's trial. He was a type of the rich and corrupt Romans of his age; a worldly-minded statesman, conscious of no higher wants than those of this life, yet by no means unmoved by feelings of justice and mercy. His conduct to the Jews in the instances given by Josephus, though severe, was not thoughtlessly cruel or tyrannical, considering the general practice of Roman governors, and the difficulties of dealing with a nation so arrogant and perverse. Certainly there is nothing in the facts recorded by profane authors inconsistent with his desire to save our Lord. But all his better feelings were overpowered by a selfish regard for his own security. He would not encounter the least hazard of personal annoyance in behalf of innocence and justice; the unrighteous condemnation of a good man was a trifle in comparison with the fear of the emperor's frown and the loss of place and power. The unhappy notoriety given to his name by its place in the two universal creeds of Christendom is due, not to any desire to singling him out for shame, but to the need of fixing the date of our Lord's death, and so bearing witness to the claims of Christianity to rest on a historical basis. That the conduct of Pilate was highly criminal can not be denied. But his guilt was light in comparison with the atrocious depravity of the Jews, especially the priests. His was the guilt of weakness and fear; theirs was the guilt of settled and deliberate malice. His state of mind prompted him to attempt the release of an accused person in opposition to the clamors of a misguided mob; theirs urged them to compass the ruin of an acquitted person by instigating the populace, calumniating the prisoner and terrifying the judge. Viewing the entire conduct of Pilate, his previous iniquities as well as his bearing on the condemnation of Jesus, viewing his own actual position and the malignity of the Jews, we can not give our vote with those who have passed the severest condemnation on this weak and guilty governor.

NOTE.—In this account we have largely availed ourselves of the article in Smith's Dict. of the Bible, with additions from McClintock & Strong, and others.

THE DEATH WARRANT OF CHRIST.

[NOTE.—The Sentence below is a translation from a Hebrew inscription on a copper-plate tablet, first discovered in A. D. 1200, while excavating for antiquities at Aquila, the site of the ancient Amiternum, whose ruins are still to be seen near St. Vittorino, 53 miles N. E. of Rome. It was subsequently brought into prominence by Dominique Vivant Denon, the great French archæologist —born at Chalon-sur-Saone, 1747, died at Paris, 1825. On the reverse side of the tablet is inscribed: "A like plate is sent to each of the tribes." For life, labors, etc., of Denon, see Encyclopedia Britannica, Vol. VII., Art. Denon.]

SENTENCE RENDERED BY PONTIUS PILATE,

THAT JESUS OF NAZARETH SHALL SUFFER DEATH ON THE CROSS.

SENTENCE.

"In the year seventeen of the empire of Tiberius Cæsar, and the 24th of March, the city of the Holy Jerusalem: Annas and Caiaphas being priests, sacrificators of the people of God, I, Pontius Pilate, governor of the prætory, condemn Jesus of Nazareth to die on the cross between two thieves—

the great and notorious evidence of the people saying—

"1. He is a seducer.

"2. He is seditious.

"3. He is the enemy of the law.

"4. He calls himself, falsely, the Son of God.

"5. He calls himself the King of Israel.

"6. He entered into the Temple, followed by a multitude bearing palm branches in their hands.

"Order the centurion, Quintius Cornelius, to lead him to the place of execution.

"Forbid any person whomsoever, poor or rich, to oppose the death of Jesus.

"The witnesses that signed the death of Jesus are:

"1. Daniel, Rabbi, Pharisee.

"2. Joannes, Rabbi.

"3. Raphael Rorobable.

"4. Capet, a citizen.

"Jesus shall go out of the city by the gate 'Struenus.'"

GESTA PILATI.

———

[The following document is a translation from the Latin text of a manuscript in the Vatican library, Rome. It has hitherto not appeared in any of the translations of the writings ascribed to Pontius Pilate. A specimen of the Latin is given in the pages immediately following the translation.]

Pontius Pilate to Tiberius Cæsar, Emperor, Sends Greeting:

The events of those last few days were of such a character in my province that I have thought I should write concerning them in detail, since I should not wonder if, in coming years, they may change the fortune of our nation; for it seems of late that the gods have ceased to be friends. It is not far from me to say, "Cursed be the day on which I succeeded Valerius Gratus in the government of Judea." When I came up to Jerusalem and occupied the Pretorium, I ordered a banquet to be splendidly prepared, to which I invited the tetrarch of Galilee with his high priests and his prefects. At the appointed time no guests were

present, which thing was an insult to my dignity.
After a few days it pleased the high priest to call
on me. He bore himself gravely and deceitfully.
He feigned that his religion forbade him and his
companions to sit down and offer up libations with
the Romans. It seemed to me politic to accept
his excuse, but from that time I was convinced that
the conquered were the professed enemies of their
conquerors. Of all the cities which had been over-
come, it appeared to me that Jerusalem was the
most difficult to be held in subjection. So turbulent were the people that I was in perpetual fear
of a sedition, for repressing which there was one
centurion only, and a small band of soldiers. I had
requested aid from the prefect of Syria, who announced to me that he had scarcely sufficient troops
for defense of his own province. I fear that the
insatiate thirst of conquering beyond what we are
able to defend shall lose to us our noble government. Among the many rumors which were borne
to my ears, one especially occupied my mind. A
young man had come into Galilee, it was said,
teaching with a noble zeal a new law in the name
of the gods who had sent him. At first I feared
his design might be to stir up the people against
the Romans; but soon my fears were borne away.
Jesus, the Nazarene, spoke more as a friend of the

Romans than of the Jews. One day going by the place of Siloam, at which there was a great concourse of people, I saw a young man in the midst of the assembly, who, leaning against a tree, calmly addressed the multitude. I was told that it was Jesus. This I could have easily suspected, such was the difference between him and his hearers. His hair and beard, of golden yellow, gave a celestial aspect. He appeared to be about thirty years old. Never have I seen a gentler or more serene countenance. What a difference between him and those listening, with their black beards and tawny complexions. Since I was unwilling to interrupt him by my presence, I pursued my walking, but gave a sign to my secretary that he should draw near to the crowd and listen. The name of my secretary was Manlius. He was the grandson of the leader of the conspirators, who were encamped in Etruria awaiting Cataline. · Manlius was an old inhabitant of Judea, and knew the Hebrew language well. He was devoted to me, and worthy of my confidence. On entering the Pretorium, I found Manlius, who related to me the words spoken at Siloam. Never have I heard from the Portico nor in the works of the philosophers, anything that can be compared with the maxims of Jesus. When a certain one of the rebellious Jews,

who are so numerous in Jerusalem, asked him
whether it were lawful to give tribute to Cæsar,
Jesus answered: "Render unto Cæsar the things
which are his, and unto God the things which are
God's."

It was on account of the wisdom of this saying that I granted so much liberty to the Nazarene, for it was in my power to have him arrested
and exiled to Pontus; but this would have been
contrary to the justice which has always character-
ized the Romans. This man was neither seditious
nor rebellious. I extended to him my protection,
unknown, perhaps, to himself. He was at liberty
to act, to speak, to assemble and address the
people, to choose disciples, unrestrained by any
pretorian mandate. Should it ever happen—may
the gods avert the omen—I say should it ever happen that the religion of our ancestors be supplanted by the religion of Jesus, it will be to this
noble toleration that Rome shall owe her prema-
ture obsequies; while I, miserable wretch, shall
have been the instrument of what the Hebrews
call providence, and we, destiny.

But this unlimited freedom granted to Jesus provoked the Jews; not the poor, but the rich and
powerful. It is true that Jesus was severe on the
latter; and this was a political reason, in my opin-

ion, why I should not control the liberty of the
Nazarene. "Scribes and Pharisees," he would say
to them, "you are a race of the vilest sort. You
are like painted sepulchres." At other times he
would deride the proud alms of the publican, saying to him that the mite of the widow was greater
in the eye of God. New complaints were made
daily at the Pretorium concerning the insolence of
Jesus. I was even informed that some misfortune
would befall him; that it would not be the first
time that Jerusalem had stoned those who called
themselves prophets, and that if the Pretorium
should refuse justice, appeal would be made to
Cæsar. Nevertheless, my conduct was pleasing to
the Senate, and I was promised aid after the Par-
thian war was ended. Since I was too weak to
suppress a sedition, I resolved upon a plan to give
quiet to the city, yet not to lay aside the authority
of the Pretorium. I sent a message to Jesus,
desiring that he should come to me at the Pretorium. You know that the Spanish blood mixed
with the Roman blood is in my veins, equally
incapable of fear and childish emotion. When the
Nazarene made his appearance, I was walking in
my basilic, and my feet seemed fastened with an
iron hand to the marble pavement, and I trembled
in every limb as a culprit, while he was calm—the

Nazarene—calm as innocence. When he came up
to me he stopped, and by a sign seemed to say, "I
am here." For awhile I contemplated with ad-
miration and awe this extraordinary type of man
unknown to the many painters who have given
form and figure to all the gods and heroes.

"Jesus," said I to him at length, and my tongue
faltered, "Jesus of Nazareth, I have granted you
for the last three years ample freedom of speech,
nor do I regret it. Your words are those of a
sage. I know not whether you have read Socrates
and Plato; but this I do know, that there is in
your discourses a majestic simplicity that elevates
you far above these philosophers. The emperor
is informed of it, and I, his humble representative
in this country, am glad of having allowed the
liberty of which you are so worthy. However, I
must not conceal from you that your discourses
have raised up against you powerful and inveterate
enemies. Nor is this surprising. Socrates had his
enemies, and he fell a victim to their hatred.
Yours are doubly incensed against you, on account
of your sayings and on account of the liberty extended towards you. They even accuse me of
being indirectly leagued with you for the purpose
of depriving the Hebrews of the little civil power
which Rome has left them. My *request*—I do not

say my order—is, that you be more circumspect in
the future, and more tender in arousing the pride
of your enemies, lest they raise against you the
stupid populace, and compel me to employ the
instruments of justice."

The Nazarene calmly replied: "Prince of the
earth, your words proceed not from true wisdom.
Say to the torrent, stop in the midst of the mountain home, because it will uproot the trees of the
valley. The torrent will answer you that it must
obey the laws of the Creator. God alone knows
whither flows the torrent. Verily, I say unto you,
before the rose of Sharon blossoms the blood of
the just shall be spilt."

"Your blood shall not be spilt," replied I, with
emotion. "You are more precious in my estima-
tion, on account of your wisdom, than all the
turbulent and proud Pharisees, who abuse the freedom granted them by the Romans, conspire
against Cæsar and construe our bounty into fear.
Insolent wretches, they are not aware that the
wolf of the woods sometimes clothes himself with
the skin of the sheep. I will protect you against
them. My Pretorium is open to you as an asylum."

Jesus carelessly shook his head, and with a grace
and a divine smile said: "When the day shall

have come, there will be no asylum for the Son of
Man, neither in the earth nor under the earth.
The asylum of the just is there" (pointing to the
heavens). "That which is written in the books of
the prophets must be accomplished."

"Young man," answered I mildly, "you oblige
me to convert my request into an order. The
safety of the province which is confided to my
care requires it. You *must* observe more modera-
tion in your discourses. Do not infringe. My
orders, you know. May happiness attend you.
Farewell."

"Prince of earth," replied Jesus, "I come not to
bring war into the world, but peace, love and char-
ity. I was born the same day on which Augustus
Cæsar gave peace to the Roman world. Persecu-
tion proceeds not from me. I expect it from
others, and will meet it in obedience to the will of
my Father, who has shown me the way. Restrain,
therefore, you worldly prudence. It is not in your
power to arrest the victim at the foot of the taber-
nacle of expiation." So saying he disappeared
like a bright shadow behind the curtains of the
basilic.

To Herod, who then reigned in Galilee, the
enemies of Jesus addressed themselves, to wreak
their vengeance on the Nazarene. Had Herod

consulted his own inclination, he would have ordered Jesus immediately to be put to death; but though proud of his royal dignity, yet he was afraid of committing an act that might diminish his influence with the Senate. Herod called on me one day at the Pretorium, and on rising to take his leave, after some insignificant conversation, he asked me what was my opinion concerning the Nazarene. I replied that Jesus appeared to be one of those great philosophers that great nations sometimes produce, that his doctrines are by no means sacrilegious, and that the intention of Rome was to leave him to that freedom of speech which was justified by his actions. Herod smiled maliciously, and saluting me with an ironical respect, he departed. The great feast of the Jews was approaching, and their intention was to avail themselves of the popular exultation which always manifests itself at the solemnities of the Passover. The city was overflowing with a tumultuous populace clamoring for the death of the Nazarene. My emissaries informed me that the treasure of the Temple had been employed in bribing the people. The danger was pressing. A Roman centurion had been insulted. I had written to the prefect of Syria for a hundred foot-soldiers and as many

4

cavalry. He had declined. I saw myself alone
with a handful of veterans in the midst of a rebellious city, too weak to suppress a disorder, and
having no other choice left but to tolerate it.
They had seized upon Jesus, and the seditious
rabble, although they had nothing to fear from the
Pretorium, believing, with their leaders, that I
winked at their sedition, continued vociferating,
"Crucify him! crucify him?" Three powerful
parties had combined together at that time against
Jesus. First, the Herodians and the Saducees,
whose seditious conduct seemed to have proceeded
from double motives. They hated the Nazarene,
and were impatient of the Roman yoke. They
could never forgive me for having entered their
holy city with banners that bore the image of the
Roman emperor, and, although in this instance I
had committed a fatal error, yet the sacrilege did
not appear less heinous in their eyes. Another
grievance, also, raukled in their bosoms. I had
proposed to employ a part of the treasure of the
Temple in erecting edifices of public utility. My
proposal was scowled at. The Pharisees were the
avowed enemies of Jesus. They cared not for the
government. They bore with bitterness the severe
reprimands which the Nazarene for three years
had been throwing out against them wherever he

had gone. Too weak and pusilanimous to act by themselves, they had embraced the quarrels of the Herodians and the Sadducees. Besides these three parties I had to contend against the reckless and profligate populace, always ready to join a sedition, and to profit by the disorder and confusion that followed from it. Jesus was dragged before the high priest and condemned. It was there that the high priest Caiaphas performed a derisory act of submission. He sent his prisoner to me to pronounce his condemnation to death and secure his execution. I answered him that as Jesus was a Galilean, the affair came in Herod's jurisdiction, and ordered him to be sent thither. The wily tetrarch professed humility, and protesting his preference to the Lieutenant of Cæsar, he committed the fate of the man to my hands. Soon my palace assumed the aspect of a beseiged citadel. Every moment increased the number of the seditionists. Jerusalem was inundated with crowds from the mountains of Nazareth. All Judea appeared to be pouring into the devoted city. I had taken a wife—a girl from among the Gauls, who pretended to see into futurity, weeping and throwing herself at my feet—"Beware," said she to me, "beware and touch not that man, for he is holy. Last night I saw him in a vision. He

was walking on the waters. He was flying on the
wings of the winds. He spoke to the tempest and
to the fishes of the lake; all were obedient to him.
Behold! the torrent in Mount Kedron flows with
blood, the statues of Cæsar are filled with the filth
of Gemoniæ, the columns of the Interium have
given away and the sun is veiled in mourning like
a vestal in the tomb. O, Pilate, evil awaits thee
if thou wilt not listen to the prayers of thy wife.
Dread the curse of the Roman Senate, dread the
powers of Cæsar."

By this time the marble stairs groaned under
the weight of the multitude. The Nazarene was
brought back to me. I proceeded to the hall of
justice, followed by my guard, and asked the people in a severe tone what they demanded. "The
death of the Nazarene," was their reply. "For
what crime?" "He has blasphemed. He has
prophesied the ruin of the Temple. He calls himself the Son of God, the Messiah, the King of the
Jews." "Roman justice," said I, "punishes not
such offenses with death." "Crucify him, crucify
him!" belched forth the relentless rabble. The
vociferations of the infuriated mob shook the palace to its foundations. There was but one who
appeared to be calm in the midst of the vast multitude. It was the Nazarene. After many fruit-

less attempts to protect him from this fury of his merciless persecutors, I adopted a measure which at the moment appeared to me to be the only one that could save his life. I ordered him to be scourged; then calling for an ewer, I washed my hands in the presence of the multitude, thereby signifying to them my disapproval of the deed. But in vain. It was his life that these wretches thirsted for.

Often in our civil commotions have I witnessed the furious animosity of the multitude, but nothing could be compared to what I witnessed in the present instance. It might have been truly said that on this occasion all the phantoms of the infernal regions had assembled at Jerusalem. The multitude appeared not to walk. It was borne off and whirled as a vortex, rolling along like living waves from the portals of the Pretorium even unto Mount Zion, with howlings such as were never heard in the seditions of the Panonia, or in the tumults of the forum. By degrees the day darkened like a winter's twilight, such as had been at the death of the great Julius Cæsar. It was likewise towards the ides of March. I, the continued governor of a rebellious province, was leaning against a column of my basalic contemplating through the dreary gloom these fiends of torture dragging to execution the innocent Nazarene. All around me was deserted. Jerusalem had vomited forth her indwellers through the funeral gate that leads to the Gemonica. An air of desolation and sadness enveloped me. My guards had joined the cavalry, and the centurion, to display a shadow of power, was endeavoring to keep order. I was left alone, and my breaking heart admonished me that what was passing at that moment appertained rather to the history of the gods than to that of man. A loud clamor was heard proceeding from Golgotha, which, borne on the winds, seemed to announce an agony such as had never been heard by mortal ears. Dark clouds lowered over the pinnacle of the Temple, and, settling over the city, covered it as with a veil. So dreadful were the signs that were seen, both in the heavens and on the earth, that Dionysius, the Areopagite, is reported to have exclaimed, "Either the author of nature is suffering, or the universe is falling apart." Toward the first hour of the night I threw my mantle around me and went down into the city toward the gates of Golgotha. The sacrifice was consummated. The multitude was returning home; still agitated, it is true, but gloomy, taciturn and desperate. What it had witnessed had caused terror and remorse. I also saw my little Roman cobort pass by mournfully, the standard-bearer having veiled his eagle in token of grief, and I overheard some of the soldiers murmuring strange words, which I did not understand. Others were recounting prodigies almost similar to those which had so often smitten the Romans by the will of the gods. Sometimes groups of men and women would halt, then looking back towards Golgotha would remain motionless, in expectation of witnessing some new prodigy. I returned to the Pretorium, sad and pensive. On ascending the stairs, the steps of which were still stained with the blood of the Nazarene, I perceived an old man in a suppliant posture, and behind him several women in tears. He threw himself at my feet and wept bitterly. It is painful to see an old man weep.

"Father," said I to him mildly, "who are you, and what is your request?"

"I am Joseph of Arimathea," replied he, "and am come to beg of you upon my knees the permission to bury Jesus of Nazareth."

"Your prayer is granted," said I to him, and at the same time ordered Manlius to take some soldiers with him to superintend the interment, lest it should be profaned.

A few days after, the sepulchre was found empty.

His disciples published all over the country that Jesus had risen from the dead, as he had foretold. A last duty remained for me to perform, and that was to communicate to Cæsar these deplorable events. I did it on the same night that followed the fatal catastrophe, and had just finished the communication when day began to dawn. At that moment the sound of clarions playing the air of Diana struck my ear. Casting my eye toward the Cæsarean gate I beheld a troop of soldiers, and heard at a distance other trumpets sounding Cæsar's march. It was the reinforcement that had been promised me—two thousand chosen troops— who, to hasten their arrival, had marched all night. "It has been decreed by the fates," cried I, wringing my hands, "that the great iniquity should be accomplished; that for averting the deeds of yesterday troops should arrive to-day. Cruel destiny, how thou sportest with the affairs of mortals." It was but too true what the Nazarene had exclaimed while writhing on the cross, "All is consummated."

GESTA PILATI.

[Specimen of the Latin Text of the foregoing translation.—Ed.]

Pontius Pilatus salutem dicit Tiberio Imperatori : Illorum ultimorum dierum paucorum res in provincia mea ejusmodi erant, ut me de singulis rebus ordine scripturum esse putaverim, quum non miraturus sim si in volventibus annis gentis nostrae fortunas mutent; nam deos esse amicos desiisse nuper videtur. Haud multum abest quin dicam. Sit execranda dies qua Valerio Grato in Judaeae imperio successerim.

Quum ad Hierosolyma venissem et Praetorium occupavissem epulas splendide instrui jussi ad quas Galilaeae tetrarchen cum pontifice praefectisque suis vocavi. Tempore constituto nulli convivae aderant; quod dignitati meae contumelia fuit. Paucis post diebus me convenire pontifici placuit. Graviter et fraudulenter se gessit. Simulavit religionem suam vetare se comitesque cum Romanis recumbere et libare. Excusationem accipere mihi

(57)

utile videbatur; sed eo tempore victos se inimicos
victorum professos esse, mihi persuasum fuit. Om-
nium urbium quae superatae essent, Hierosolyma
in ditione difficillime teneri mihi videbantur.
Adeo turbulenti populi fuerunt ut in seditionis
metu perpetuo essem; ad quem comprimendam
mihi unus centurio et exigua militum manus fuit.

Inter complures rumores qui ad aures meas
afferrebantur, unus maxime animum occupabat.
Juvenis in Galilaeam advenisse dicebatur, legem
novam nobili fervore docens deorum nomine qui
eum mississent.

Die quodam locum Siloae praeteriens qua mag-
nus populi concursus erat juvenem in media turba
videbam, qui arbori innisus multitudinem tran-
quille alloquebatur. Jesum esse certior factus sum.
Quod facile suspicatus essem tanto fuit distantia
inter eum et audientes. Comae barbaque flavae

speciei aspectum coelestem dabant. Fere triginta
annos natus videbatur. Nunquam vultum lenio-
rem aut tranquilliorem vidi. Quanta dissimilitudo
inter eum et audientes barbis nigris coloreque
fulvo. Quum eum praesentia mea interrumpere
nollem, ambulationem persequebar; sed scribae
meo signum dabam ut ad turbam appropinquaret
atque auscultaret.

Quum in Praetorium venissem Man-
lium inveni, qui mihi quae verba Jesus Siloae pro-
nuntiavisset narravit. Nunquam in Porticu nec in
philosophorum operibus quidquam audivi quod
cum Jesu praeceptis comparari possit. Jesus, quum
quidam ex Judaeis seditiosis, quorum tot Hierosolymis erant ab eo an Caesari tributum pendere liceret
quaesivisset respondit: "Quae Caesaris sint, illi
reddite, et Deo, quae Dei sint." Cujus dicti propter sapientiam, Nazareno tantam libertatem con-
cessi, nam in potestate mea fuit ut ille compre-
hensus et in exsilium Pontum actus esset: sed id
contra justitiam fuisset quae Romanorum semper
fuit. Hic nec seditiosus, nec novarum rerum
cupidus erat. Fidem meam forsitan nescienti

dedi. In libertate erat agere loqui, populum con-
vocare et sermonem habere discipulos deligere,
nullo praetoris jussu coercitus. Siquando fiat—
utinam dii omen semper avertaut siquando inquam
fiat, ut majorum religio a Jesu religione subver-
tatur, haec nobilis indulgentia Romae exsequiarum
praematurarum causae erit, dum ego miserrime
instrumentum fuero cujus Hebraei providentiam
nos fatum nominamus.

"Scribae Pharisaeique eis dicebat homines
nequissimi estis; pictis sepulchris similes estis."

Alias superba publicani beneficia deridebat, ei
dicens pauperis viduae in Dei oculis pluris esse.

Novae querimoniae de Jesu insolentia ad Praetorium in dies factae sunt.

Etiam certior factus sum aliquam calamitatem ei
accisurum esse—non Hierosolyma nunc primum
lapides in eos conjectura esse, qui prophetas se ap-
pellarent—atque ad Caesarem provocatum iri si
Praetorium jus negavisset. Tamen procuratio mea
senatui placuit atque auxilia mihi promissa sunt
post bellum Parthorum quam finitum esset.

Quam copiis inferior essem quam ut seditionem comprimere possem, consilium inire urbe quietem firmaturum neque Praetorii auctoritatem demissurum constitui.

Literas ad Jesum misi ab eo petens ut me ad Praetorium conveniret.

Scis sanguinem Hispaniensem cum Romano mixtum aeque timoris ac ineptiarum impatientem, in venis meis manare.

Quum me adiret constitit et mihi signo dicere videbatur, "adsum." Aliquamdiu hoc insigne hominis exemplum admiratione venerationeque contemplabar—hominis exemplum multis pictoribus nostris ignarum qui formam figuramque omnibus diis heroibusque dederunt. "Jesus" denique ei dicebam, et lingua haerebat "Jesus Nazarenus jam tres tibi annos summam liberatem in oratione dedi, neque me poenitet. Verba tua sapientis sunt. Nescio utrum Socratem an Platonem legeris, sed hoc scio, in sermonibus tuis simplicitatem augustam esse, quae te multo super hos philosophos tollit.

De his rebus Imperator certior factus est, et ego

qui ejus vicem in hac regione modeste impleo, gaudeo quod tibi eam libertatem qua tam dignus es dederim. Tamen, mihi non licet te celare surmones tuos tibi inimicos magnos confirmatosque creavisse.

Nec hoc mirandum est. Socrates inimicos suos habuit, et eorum odium victima cecidit. Vestri in sese dicta tua et propter libertatem tibi datam in te dupliciter incensi sunt. Etiam me incusaverunt quod tecum foedus oblique fecissem, Hebraeos exiguae potestatis civilis privandi causae, quam Roma eis permiserit. Preces meae—non imperium dico—sunt ut in posterum prudentior sis, et lenior inimicorum superbiam movendo, ne populum stultum in te excitent et me cogant ut justitiae instrumentis utar."

"Sanguis tuus non profundetur," motus respondi. Propter sapientam aestimatione mea pretiosior es quam omnes Pharisaei turbulenti superbique, qui libertate, sibi data a Romanis abutautur, in Cæsarem conjurent, et munificentiam nostram in timorem interpretentur. Homines insolentes, nesciunt lupum —— ovis pellem interdum induere. Ab eis te defendam. Praetorium meum tibi asylum patet. Asylum sanctum est. Jesus capite negligenter nutabat, et leniter divineque subridens, dixit. "Quum dies venerit, mortali matre nato, nec in terra, nec sub terra asylum erit. Ibi justorum asylum est, digito demonstrans coelum.

"Princeps terrae," Jesus respondit, "non venio, ut in terram bellum, sed pacem, amorem, caritatemque feram. Eodem die, quo Augustus Cæsar pacem Populo Romano dedit, natus sum. Vexatio a me non procedit. Eam ab aliis expecto, et secundum patris mei voluntatem, ei obviam ibo, qui mihi viam monstravit. Coerce, ergo, providentiam terrestriam. Tibi non licet, ut victimam sub expiationis tabernaculo comprehendas."

Haec locutus, similes lucidae umbrae, post basi-

licae vela evanuit. Jesu inimici Herodem, qui in
Galilaea tum regnabat, aggressi sunt, ut Nazrenum
ulciscerentur. Si Herodes egisset pro eo ac voluit,
Jesum statim necari jussisset; sed quamquam in
dignitate regia superbus, tamen aliquam rem facere
timuit, qua se apud senatum minus valeret. Quodam die Herodes ad Praetorium me convenit, et
surgens ut salvere me juberet, quibusdam nugis
interjectis, a me quaesivit, quid de Nazareno senti-
rem.

Magnum Judaeorum sollemne aderat, et in
animo habebant ut populi exsultatione, quae
semper se praebet in paschae sollennitatibus,
uterentur. Urbs turba tumultuosa, Nazareni mortem flagitante, abundabat. Speculatores mei cer-
tiorem me fecerunt templi copias in populis
corrumpendis adhibitas esse. Periculum impen-
debat. Centurio Romanus contumelia affectus
erat. Ad Syriae praefectum literas misi, centum
pedites et totidem equites rogatum. Negavit. Me
solum, cum exigua veteranorum manu, in media

urbe seditiosa vidi, debilior quam ut perturbationem comprimere possem, cum nulla optione quin tolerarem. Jesum comprehenderant; et turba seditiosa, quamquam Praetorium nihil timebant, ducibus ductoribus, credens me tumultum connivere, vociferabat, "Eum crucia! eum crucia!" Tres potentes factiones in Jesum tum se junxerant. Primum, Herodiani Sadducaeique, quorum seditio duabus causis processisse videbatur.

Alia molestia, etiam, in animis incensa est. Animo intenderam ut parte templi copiarum, in aedificiis publicis exstruendis, uterer. Propositum meum animo infesto audiebatur. Pharisaei Jesu inimici professi erant. Imperium negligebant. Reprehensiones acres, quas Nazarenus in eos, ubicumque iret, jam tres annos jactabat, graviter ferebant. Debiliores infirmioresque quam ut soli agere possent, ad Herodianorum et Sadducaeorum controversias inierant. Praeter has tres factiones, mihi contra turbam praecipitem perditamque contendendum erat, ad

5

seditionem jungendum semper paratam, et ad tumultus perturbationisque fructum capiendum, qui ab ea sequeretur.

Jesus ad pontificem captus est, et capitis damnatus est. Caiaphas, pontifex, deridens, tum se subjecit. Ad me captiorum misit ut eum capitis damnarem, et morte afficerem. Ad eum respondi, quum Jesus Galilaeus esset, rem penes Herodem esse, atque eo mitti jussi. Tetrarches callidus submisse se gerere simulabat, et asseverans se Caesaris legatum anteponere, mihi hominis fortunam commisit. Brevi tempore palatium meum arcis obsessae speciem sumpsit.

Suprema nocte in somnis eum vidi. In undis ambulabat. In ventis volabat. Tempestates, lacus, piscesque alloquebatur—omnia ei pasuerunt. Ecce torrens in monte Cedrone cruore fluit, Caesaris imagines Gemoniarum illuvie plena sunt, columnae Interii cesserunt, et sol in luctu similis vestae in sepulchro, velatus est. O Pilate! malum tibi impendet,

nisi conjugis vota audias. Senatus Romani impre-
cationes metue, metue Cæsaris vires."

.   .

"Naza-
reni mortem," responderunt. Cujus sceleris
causa?" "Blasphemia usus est. Templi ruinam-
praedixit. Dei Filium, Messiam, Judaeorum Regem,
se appellat.' "Romanorum justitia," dixi, offem
siones tales morte non vindicat.' "Eum crucia,
eum crucia!" clamabat vulgus saevum. Turbae
iratae vociferationes palatium funditis concusse-
runt. Unus placidus in media multitudine vasta
videbatur. Nazarenus erat.

Eum virgis ver-
berari jussi; deinde urnam postulans, coram multitudine, manus lavi, ea re iis facti reprehensionem
significans. Sed nequidquam. Hi miseri victam
sitiebant. Saepe in motibus civilibus, saevum
multitudinis odium vidi, sed nihil iis rebus comparari potiut quas eo tempore vidi. Vere dictum
esset omnia infernorum spectra Hierosolymis con-
venisse. Turba non ambulari videbatur. Rapieba-
tur, et volvebatur ut vortex, convolvens veluti undae

vivae, a Praetorii portis usque ad Montem Sion,
cum ejulatibus, clamoribus, ululatibus, vocifera-
tiouibusque, talibus quales in Panoniae seditionibus
nunquam audiebantur, nec in Fori tumultu.

Ego, continuus provinciae seditiosae procurator,
basilicae columuae me acclinabam, per tenebras
moestas hos cruciatus daemonas contemplatus
Nazarenum innocentem ad mortem rapientes.
Omnia circum me deserta fuerunt. Hierosolyma
per portam funebrem ad Gemonicam ducentem
incolas evomuerant. Solitudinis tristitiaeque sensus
me circumstetit. Satellites mei equitatum junxerant, et centurio, ut potentiae speciem praeberet,
ordinem tenere conabatur. Solus relictus sum, et
animus sollicitus me admonuit quae tum agerentur
magis ad deorum historiam quam hominum perti-
nere.

Nubes densae templi culmen oc-
cultabant, et urbi imminentes velamento texerunt.
Signa et coelo et terra visa tam dira fuerunt, ut
Dionysius Areopagites clamavisse feratur, "Aut
naturae auctor patitur, aut universum proruit."

Fere prima noctis hora mihi pallium circumjeci,. et in urbem, ad Golgotha portas degressus sum. Sacrificium finitum est. Turba domum rediebat; adhuc agitatus vero; sed moesta, taciturna, desperata. Quae viderant, eos terrore scelerumque conscientia percusserant. Parvam cohortem Romanam moeste praeterire etiam vidi, quum signifer, dolorem significans, acquilam velavisset, et auribus verba mira excepi, a quibusdam militibus jacta, quae non intellexi. Alii prodigia prope similia eis quae Romanos tam saepe icerant, deorum voluntate, narrabant. Interdum hominum feminarumque turbae stabant, tum adversus Golgotha respicientes, immotae manebant, expectantes quoddam novum prodigium videre.

"Pater," ad eum leniter dixi, "quis es, et quid petis?"

"Arimatheae Josephus sum," respondit, "et ad te veni, in genibus petitum, ut mihi liceat Jesum Nazrenum sepelire."

"Supplicatio concessa est," ad eum dixi, et simul

Manlium jussi secum aliquos milites ducere, qui
sepulturae praesssent, ne violaretur.

Paucis post diebus, sepulchrum vacuum inven-
tum est. Discipuli per tatem rigionem pronuntia-
bant Jesum in vitam rediisse, ut praedixisset.
Officium ultimum mihi manebat ut ad te de his
rebus miserandis perscriberem. Quod eadem nocte
feci, quae fatalem catastropham secuta est, et
literas vix perfeceram, quum lucesceret. "Eo ipso
tempore, lituorum sonus, canticum Dianae canen-
tium, ad aures meas pervenit. Quum oculos ad
portam Cæsariensem vertissem, militum turmam
vidi, et procul alias tubas, Cæsaris classicum
·canantes, audivi.

"Fatis decretum est," clamabam, manus torquens,
"ut nefas immane conficiatur; ut ad hesterna facta
avertendum, milites hodie veniant! Fatum cru-
·dele, quomodo hominum res illudis!" Niminum
·vera, quae Nazarenus, se in cruce torquens, exclam-
·abat: "Omne finitum est."

NOTES.

NOTES.

[The following notes on passages from the first pages of the foregoing report of Pilate have been made as suggestions rather to the mind of the reader as to one of the methods of analyzing the writing as to its genuineness than as exhaustive at all of the arguments pro and con that may arise in the minds of divers readers while thinking over its pages.]

" The events of those last few days."—Pilate evidently here refers to the events immediately connected with the apprehension, trial and crucifixion of Jesus; and it may be to some of the events subsequent to the crucifixion. This language was written subsequent to a former report made, as Pilate afterwards states, "on the same night that followed the fatal catastrophe."

"In detail."—This expression signifies rather a report of the main points connected with the entire case, and their bearings on its conclusion.

" Cursed be the day."—This language discovers to the reader the intense feeling of perplexity under which Pilate labored while recalling the events of those last days of the life of the Savior; and these words are certainly very natural in one situated as Pilate was at this particular time, and related as he had been to most of the events of this report.

"When I came up to Jerusalem."—This doubtless refers to the arrival of the procurator, Pilate, on or a short time before the oc-

casion of the great feast. It was customary for the Roman's procurators to go up to Jerusalem at such time for the trial of such
matters as might come before the Jewish council. And it is most
probable that Pilate went up at this time filled with the gravest
apprehensions of the results of this very trial of Jesus. For it
will be remembered by all who have paid any attention to this de-
partment of history that Jesus was by no means an insignificant
person at this time. He had, by his life and teachings, made himself not only obnoxious to orthodox Jewry as an opposer and a
destroyer of their time-honored laws and religious ceremonies, but,
in the language of to-day, was looked upon as a political reformer
and disturber, whose influence was felt and acknowledged. by the
masses of the people. And though his acts and his teaching may
have been looked upon by both Jew and Roman with much uneasy
suspicion and even dreadful apprehension, yet they had been done
with such prudence, judgment and wisdom that it was difficult to
arrest the tide of his influence except by a resort to very arbitrary
and very questionable acts on the part of either the Roman or
Jewish authorities. Whoever will inquire minutely into the exact
situation of affairs at this particular juncture will find that the
trial of Jesus was far from being one of ordinary difficulty, and
we think, moreover, will heartily sympathize with even Pilate
himself in the difficult proceedings of a court at such time and
under circumstances to which he was then called as a judge. So
much has been written, however, on this particular epoch, that we
forbear to say anything here. We shall only add that the after
remarks of Pilate to the emperor concerning the turbulence of the
people of Jerusalem—the grave, well studied deceit of their
priests, and the insults which they offered him—are sufficient to
show his frame of mind in regard to the present situation, and the
great difficulties he had to contend with in the conduct of this
great trial of Jesus, which the Jewish priesthood had determined

upon, and the results of which they were equally determined to secure.

"I ordered a banquet to be splendidly prepared."—Pilate was at this time not the most popular governor among the Jews. He had committed several acts of a character very offensive to them in the former years of his administration. The most natural and politic thing for him to do, therefore, as a shrewd politician, was to court the friendship of the Jewish leaders and officials. And as nothing is better calculated to soften and conciliate men of this type than social feasting, this banquet seems to have been a happy and very natural thought in the mind of Pilate. The Jews, however, seem to have been quite as skillful in political tact as the governor himself, on this occasion at least, and refused to be brought into any such relation as seems to have been in the mind of the Governor Pilate to induce. This appears very fully from the language used immediately after by Pilate : He "*feigned* that his religion forbade him," etc. This, at least seems to have been Pilate's view concerning the Jews' refusal to accept his invitation, although the "excuse" offered by the high priest may have been sincere and most proper.

"He feigned that his religion forbade him and his attendants to sit down and offer up libations with the Romans."—This sentence is almost conclusive evidence of this report's having been written by Pilate, and not by some Christian afterward fabricating or counterfeiting that report. Pilate, if honest in this statement, must have been ignorant of the Jewish law forbidding the Jews to "sit down and offer up libations with the Romans" to heathen gods, or he could not have accused the priest of "feigning." If he was acquainted with the law, then he himself was deceiving the emperor in making this false accusation against the high priest; and did it simply to arouse the feelings of Tiberius against the

Jewish priesthood.   And it occurs to us that a writer fabricating a report would, most probably, never have thought of so minute a point in the mind of Pilate as the ignorance of a mere item in the religious statutes of the Jewish laws.   This sentence bears, we think, very conclusive evidence of having been written by none other than Pilate himself.

" It seemed to me politic to accept his excuse."—Pilate seems determined, by every statement made in this immediate connection, to carry his point with the emperor as against the Jewish priests.   His charge against the high priest of grave and well-studied deceit in manner on his visit, of his feigning or lying about not attending the feast, and of his (Pilate's) being compelled from good policy to accept the "excuse" or lie of the high priest, are all laid down as premises to the conclusion which Pilate would impress on the mind of Tiberius, viz: "*that the conquered were the enemies of the conquerors*," and that this was especially the case in Jerusalem, the stage upon which had been played this terrible drama, now big with omens of equally terrible results to the Roman government in Judea.

It will be remembered by the reader that this was a leading feature in this great trial of Jesus, as related to Pilate and the Jewish priesthood, viz: the settlement of the question as to "who was Cæsar's friend in this matter;" and Pilate is still at work in the settlement of this question by laying before the emperor the exact position of himself, as also of the priesthood as related to the entire matter.

"The conquered were the professed enemies," etc.—The main transaction, the chief event of this report, certainly, is the crucifixion of the Nazarene Jesus; and the main design of its writer at this point in the report certainly was to create in the mind of the reader a sentiment against the leading Jews and favorable to

Pilate, so far as that transaction was concerned. For, although Pilate had done in the matter of condemning Jesus to death what was well pleasing to these chief men among the Jews, yet he had done what was equally displeasing to the masses, perhaps. He was tired of appeals to Cæsar, doubtless, and feared the very threat of them, from whatever class or source they might come. He feared this threat from the chief priests before the crucifixion, and it may be that he now feared it from certain of the friends of Jesus. The tide of public opinion is a fearful tide to rulers, and political rulers watch it closely. The tide, which was before his death *against* Jesus, may now have changed or showed signs of a change *for* Jesus. If so, Pilate could lose no time, in his situation, in making ready and meeting anything sent to Rome against himself.

"I fear that the insatiate thirst of conquering," etc.—This complaint against the policy of the Roman government as not being a wise policy comes very naturally from a ruler in Pilate's present situation, and could have been penned only by one in such situation actually and really, as was the Procurator Pilate. If this language be the composition of a Romish priest, monk or other counterfeiter of Pilate's, who was fabricating a piece of history in behalf and in interest of Christian evidences on the divinity of Jesus Christ, truly he has exhibited in these few sentences very remarkable skill and ingenuity of invention while painting the mind of Pilate when writing to his emperor. We do not say that it is impossible, but we must say it is improbable that such a writer on such a subject should have thought of such an interest in the general governmental policy of heathen Rome as is here manifested as existing in Pilate's mind. These simple, straightforward, plain statements of sentiment are made, moreover, without any argument or comment on the part of the writer, and without any attempt to expand or enlarge upon their importance.

They may bear signs of spuriousness to the minds of acuter think-
ers and critics, but to our mind nothing of this character appears
in them. Our comments upon them have been made more
through a desire to have the reader weigh them critically than
through any wish to impress upon him the correctness of our
conclusions in regard to the passages which form the text of our
notes.

"One day in passing by the place of Siloam."—The place of
Siloam may refer to the site of an ancient village of this name, or
the Pool. Our Lord mentions the tower of Siloam, but no further
mention is made of it in the Scripture account. The reader will
find a full account of the Pool and all that is known of it in
Smith's Dictionary of the Bible, or in my old friend Dr. Barclay's
explorations in and around Jerusalem, as given in his "City of the
Great King." What we wished to refer to particularly is the fact
that this discourse of Jesus is not mentioned in the accounts given
by the Evangelists, and could not have been taken from their nar-
ratives by the writer of the sentence in our text. This place of
Siloam seems to have been in the days of the Savior a resort for
those who might be taking in the scenes in and around the holy
city. Pilate seems to have been walking more for this reason than
any other at the time of his coming upon the multitude assembled
about Jesus. And believing, doubtless, that Jesus was discoursing
to the people on matters that pertained to political affairs proceeds
with his walking, but leaves Manlius to investigate the matter and
report to him on his return to the palace. It must be observed
here that, so far, Pilate shows conclusively that the thought upper-
most in his mind was as to the offense against the Roman government by Jesus, as reported by the Jews in their charge against him
as a political offender. He cared not for any religious dispute
that might be in agitation as between Jesus and the high priests,
but he *did care*, as it was his business to do, for any political

agitation that might be the design of Jesus to raise up, and he therefore "walked on," and left Manlius to hear and report, as being the easiest method of finding out the real sentiments of the Savior, should he express any, in relation to political or governmental affairs. The sentences immediately following show this very plainly. And, from all we know concerning the Savior on these points, so narrowly watched by the governor of Judea, Pilate has here given the truth as to the mind and expressions of the Lord in regard to the feelings he exercised toward his Roman masters.

PART II.

THE

REPORTS, LETTERS AND ACTS

OF

PONTIUS PILATE:

BEING A TRANSLATION FROM TISCHENDORF.

AS MADE BY

ALEXANDER WALKER, ESQ.,

ONE OF HER MAJESTY'S INSPECTORS OF SCHOOLS FOR SCOTLAND.

REPORT OF PILATE THE PROCURATOR,

CONCERNING OUR LORD JESUS CHRIST, SENT TO
THE AUGUST CÆSAR IN ROME.

FIRST FORM.

In those days, our Lord Jesus Christ having
been crucified under Pontius Pilate, Procurator of
Palestine and Phœnicia, these records were made
in Jerusalem as to what was done by the Jews
against the Lord.   Pilate, therefore, along with his
private report, sent them to Cæsar in Rome, writing
thus: To the most mighty, venerable, most divine
and most terrible, the august Cæsar, Pilate, the
governor of the East, sends greeting.   I have, O
most mighty, a narrative to give thee, on account
of which I am seized with fear and trembling, for
in this government of mine, of which one of the
cities is called Jerusalem, all the people of the
Jews have delivered to me a man named Jesus,
bringing many charges against him which they
were not able to convict him of by the consistency

83

of their evidence. And one of the heresies they
had against him was that Jesus said that their
Sabbath should not be a day of leisure, and should
not be observed. For he performed many cures
on that day; he made the blind receive their sight,
the lame walk; he raised up the dead, he cleansed
the lepers; he healed paralytics that were not at
all able to make any movement of their body or
keep their nerves steady, but who had only speech
and the modulation of their voice, and he gave
them the power of walking and running, removing
their illness by a single word. Another thing
again, more powerful still, which is strange even
with our gods: he raised up one that had been
dead four days, summoning him by a single word,
when the dead man had his blood corrupted, and
when his body was destroyed by the worms produced in it, and when it had the stink of a dog.
And seeing him lying in the tomb he ordered him
to run. Nor had he anything of a dead body
about him at all; but as a bridegroom from the
bridal chamber, so he came forth from the tomb
filled with very great fragrance. And strangers
that were manifestly demoniac, and that had their
dwelling in deserts, and ate their own flesh, living
like beasts and creeping things, even these he made
to be dwellers in cities, and by his word restored

them to soundness of mind and rendered them
wise and able and reputable, eating with all the
enemies of the unclean spirits that dwelt in them
for their destruction, which he cast down into the
depths of the sea.   And again, there was another
having a withered hand; and not the hand only,
but rather the half of the body of the man was
petrified so that he had not the form of a man or
the power of moving his body.   And him, by a
word, he healed and made sound.   And a woman
that had an issue of blood for many years, and
whose joints and arteries were drained by the flowing of the blood so that she did not present the
appearance of a human being, but was like a
corpse, and was speechless every day, so that all
the physicians of the district could not cure her.
For there was not any hope of life left in her.
And when Jesus passed by she mysteriously
received strength through his overshadowing her;
and she took hold of his fringe behind, and immediately, in the same hour, power filled up in her
what was empty, so that, no longer suffering any
pain, she began to run swiftly to her own city,
Kepharnaum, so as to accomplish the journey in
six days.   And these are the things which I lately
had in my mind to report, which Jesus accomplished on the Sabbath.   And other signs greater

than these he did, so that I have perceived that the wonderlul works done by him are greater thañ can be done by the gods whom we worship. And him Herod and Archelaus and Philip, Annas and Caiaphas, with all the people, delivered to me, making a great uproar against me that I should try him. I therefore ordered him to be crucified, having first scourged him, and having found against him no cause of evil accusations or deeds. And at the time he was crucified there was darkness over all the world, the sun being darkened at mid-day and the stars appearing, but in them there appeared no lustre; and the moon, as if turned to blood, failed in her light. And the world was swallowed up by the lower regions, so that the very sanctuary of the Temple, as they call it, could not be seen by the Jews in their fall; and they saw below them a chasm of the earth, with the roar of the thunders that fell upon it. And in that terror dead men were seen that had risen, as the Jews themselves testified; and they said that it was Abraham, and Isaac and Jacob and the twelve patriarchs, and Moses and Job, that had died, as they say, three thousand five hundred years before. And there were very many whom I also saw appearing in the body; and they were making a lamentation about the Jews, on account of the wickedness that had come to pass through them, and the destruction of the Jews and their law.

And the fear of the earthquake remained from the sixth hour of the preparation until the ninth hour. And on the evening of the first day of the week there was a sound out of the heaven so that the heaven became enlightened seven-fold more than all the days. And at the third hour of the night the sun was seen brighter than it had ever shone before, lighting up the heaven. And as the lightnings came suddenly in winter so majestic, men appeared in glorious robes an innumerable multitude, whose voice was heard as that of a very great thunder, crying out: "Jesus that was crucified is risen; come up out of hades ye that have been enslaved in the underground of hades. And the chasm of the earth was as if it had no bottom; but it was as if the very foundations of the earth appeared along with those that cried out in the heavens and walked about in the body in the midst of the dead that had risen. And he that raised up all the dead and bound hades said, "Say to my disciples he goes before you into Galilee; there shall ye see him." And all that night the light did not cease shining. And many of the Jews died, swallowed up in the chasm of the earth, so

that on the following day most of those who had
been against Jesus could not be found. Others
saw the appearing of those who had risen whom
no one of us had ever seen. And only one synagogue of the Jews was left in this Jerusalem, since
all disappeared in that fall.

With that terror, being in perplexity and seized
with a most frightful trembling, I have written
what I saw at that time, and have reported to thy
majesty. Having set in order, also, what was done
by the Jews against Jesus, I have sent it, my lord,
to thy divinity.

THE REPORT OF PONTIUS PILATE,

PROCURATOR OF JUDEA.

SENT TO ROME TO TIBERIUS CÆSAR.

SECOND FORM.

To the most mighty, venerable, awful, most divine, the august, Pilatus Pontius, the governor of the East: I have to report to thy reverence through this writing of mine, being seized with great trembling and fear, O most mighty emperor, the conjuncture of the present times as the end of these things has shown. For while I, my lord, according to the commandment of thy clemency, was discharging the duties of my government, which is one of the cities of the East, Jerusalem by name, in which is built the Temple of the Jewish nation, all the multitude of the Jews came together and delivered to me a certain man named Jesus, bringing against him many groundless charges; and they were not able to convict him in anything. And one heresy against him of theirs was that he said that the Sabbath was not their right rest. And that man wrought many cures in addition to good works. He made the blind see; he cleansed the lepers; he raised the dead; he healed paralytics who could not move at all, except that they only had their voice, and the joining of their bones; and he gave them the power of walking about and running, commanding them by a single word. And another mightier work he did, which was strange even with our gods: he raised up a dead man, Lazarus, who had been dead four days, by a single word, ordering the dead man to be raised, although his body was already corrupted by worms that grow in wounds; and that ill-smelling body lying in the tomb he ordered to run; and as a bridegroom from the bridal chamber, so he came forth out of the tomb filled with exceeding fragrance. And some that were cruelly vexed by demons and had their dwellings in deserts, and ate the flesh of their own limbs, and lived along with reptiles and wild beasts, he made to be dwellers in cities in their own houses, and by a word he rendered them sound-minded, and he made those that were troubled by unclean spirits to be intelligent and reputable; and, sending away the demons in them into a herd of swine, he suffocated them in the sea. Another man, again, who had a withered hand and lived in sorrow, and had not even the half of his body sound, he rendered sound by a single word. And a woman that had a flow of blood for many years so that, in consequence of the flowing of her blood, all the joinings of her bones appeared and were transparent like glass, and assuredly all the physicians had left her without hope and had not cleansed her, for there was not in her a single hope of health; once, then, as Jesus was passing by, she took hold of the fringe of his clothes behind, and that same hour her body was completely restored to power, and she became whole as if nothing were the matter with her, and she began to run swiftly to her own city, Paneas. And these things indeed were so. And the Jews gave information that Jesus did these things on the Sabbath. And I also ascertained that the miracles done by him were greater than any which the gods whom we worship could do.

Him, then, Herod and Archelaus, and Annas and Caiaphas, with all the people, delivered to me to try him. And, as many were exciting an insurrection against me, I ordered him crucified. And when he had been crucified there was darkness over the whole earth, the sun having been completely hidden, and the heaven appearing dark,

though it was day, so that the stars appeared, but
had at the same time their brightness darkened, as
I suppose your reverence is not ignorant of, because in all the world they lighted lamps from the
sixth hour until evening. And the. moon being
like blood did not shine the whole night, and yet
she happened to be at the full. And the stars,
also, and Orion, made a lament about the Jews, on
account of the wickedness that had been done by
them. And on the first of the week, about the
third hour of the night, the sun was seen such as
it had never at any time shown, and all the heaven
was lighted up. And as lightniugs came on in
winter, so men of indescribable splendor of dress
and of glory appeared in the air, and an innumerable multitude of angels crying out and saying:
"Glory to God in the highest, and on earth peace,
among men good will; come up out of hades, ye
who have been kept in slavery in the underground
regions of hades." And at their voice all the
mountains and hills were shaken, and the rocks
were burst asunder, and great chasms were made
in the earth, so that what was also in the abyss
appeared.

And there were seen in that terror dead men
raised up, as the Jews that saw them said: "We
have seen Abraham and Isaac and Jacob, and the

twelve patriarchs that died two thousand five hundred years ago; and we have seen Noah manifestly in the body." And all the multitude walked about and sang praises to God with a loud voice, saying: "The Lord our God that has risen from the dead; has brought to life all the dead, and has plundered Hades and put him to death." All that night, therefore, my lord, O king, the light ceased not. And many of the Jews died and were engulfed and swallowed up in the chasms in that night, so that not even their bodies appeared. Those of the Jews I say suffered who had spoken against Jesus. And one synagogue was left in Jerusalem, since all the synagogues that had been against Jesus were engulfed. From that fear, then, being in perplexity and seized with much trembling, at that same hour I ordered what had been done by them to be written, and I have reported it to thy mightiness.

LETTER OF PONTIUS PILATE

TO THE ROMAN EMPEROR.

Pontius Pilate to the Emperor, Tiberius Cæsar: Upon Jesus Christ, whose case I had clearly set forth to thee in my last, at length, by the will of the people, a bitter punishment has been inflicted, myself being in a sort unwilling and rather afraid. A man, by Hercules, so pious and strict no age has ever had or will have. But wonderful were the efforts of the people themselves and the unanimity to crucify this embassador of truth, notwithstanding that their own prophets, and after our manner the sybils warned them against it; and supernatural signs appeared while he was hanging, and, in the opinion of the philosophers, threatened destruction to the whole world. His disciples are flourishing in their work, and the regulation of their lives not belying their master; yea, in his name, most beneficent. Had I not been afraid of the rising of a sedition among the people, who were just on the point of breaking out, perhaps this man would still be alive to us; although urged more by fidelity to thy dignity than induced by my own wishes, I did not, according to my strength, resist that innocent blood free from the whole charge (brought against it), but unjustly through the malignity of men, should be sold and suffer yet, as the Scriptures signify, to their own destruction. Farewell. 28th March.

LETTER OF PONTIUS PILATE

TO CLAUDIUS CÆSAR.

Pontius Pilate to Claudius, greeting: There has lately happened an event which I myself was concerned in. For the Jews, through envy, have inflicted upon themselves and on those coming after them dreadful judgments. Their fathers had promises that their God would send them his holy one from heaven, who, according to reason, should be called their king, and he had promised to send him to the earth by means of a virgin. He, then, when I was procurator, came into Judea. And they saw him enlightening the blind, cleansing lepers, healing paralytics, expelling demons from men, raising the dead, subduing the winds, walking upon the waves of the sea, and doing many other wonders, and all the people of the Jews calling him Son of God. Then the chief priests, moved with envy against him, seized him and delivered him to me; and, telling one lie after

7 (97)

another, they said he was a wizzard, and did contrary to their law. And I, having believed these things were so, gave him up, after scourging him, to their will, and they crucified him; and after he was buried set guards over him. But he, while my soldiers were guarding him, rose on the third day. And to such a degree was the wickedness of the Jews inflamed against him that they gave money to the soldiers, saying, "Say his disciples have stolen his body." But they, having taken the money, were not able to keep silence as to what had happened; for they have testified that they have seen him risen, and that they have received money from the Jews. These things have I reported, that no one should falsely speak otherwise, and that thou shouldst not suppose that the falsehoods of the Jews are to be believed.

THE ACTS OF PILATE.

THE ACTS OF PILATE.

FIRST GREEK FORM.

___

MEMORIALS OF OUR LORD JESUS CHRIST, DONE IN THE TIME OF PONTIUS PILATE.

. PROLOGUE.

I, Ananias, of the proprætor's body-guard, being
learned in the law, knowing our Lord Jesus Christ
from the Holy Scriptures, coming to him by faith,
and counted worthy of the holy baptism, searching
also the memorials written at that time of what
was done in the case of our Lord Jesus Christ,
which the Jews had laid up in the time of Pontius
Pilate, found these memorials written in Hebrew,
and, by the favor of God, have translated them
into Greek for the information of all who call
upon the name of our Master Jesus Christ, in the
seventeenth year of the reign of our lord Flavius
Theodosius, and the sixth of Flavius Valentinia-
nus, in the ninth indiction.

All ye, therefore, who read and transfer into other books, remember me and pray for me, that God may be merciful to me, and pardon my sins which I have sinned against him.

Peace be to those who read and to those who hear, and to their households.   Amen.

———

In the fifteenth year of the government of Tiberius Cæsar, emperor of the Romans, and Herod being king of Galilee, in the nineteenth year of his rule, on the eighth day before the Kalends of April, which is the 25th of March, in the consulship of Rufus and Rubellio, in the fourth year of the two hundred and second Olympiad, Joseph Caiaphas being high priest of the Jews.

The account that Nicodemus wrote in Hebrew, after the cross and passion of our Lord Jesus Christ, the Savior God, and left to those that came after him, is as follows:

CHAPTER 1.—Having called a council, the high priests and scribes Annas and Caiaphas and Semes and Dathaes, and Gamaliel, Judas, Levi and Nepthalim, Alexander and Jaïrus, and the rest of the Jews, came to Pilate accusing Jesus about many things, saying: We know this man to be the son of Joseph the carpenter, born of Mary; and he says that he is the Son of God, and a king; moreover, he profanes the Sabbath, and wishes to do away with the law of our fathers. Pilate says: And what are the things which he does, to show that he wishes to do away with it? The Jews say: We have a law not to cure any one on the Sabbath; but this man has, on the Sabbath, cured the lame and the crooked, the withered and the blind and the paralytic, the dumb and the demoniac, by evil practices. Pilate says to them: What evil practices? They say to him: He is a magician, and by Beelzebul, prince of the demons, he casts out the demons, and all are subject to him. Pilate says to them: This is not casting out the demons by an unclean spirit, but by the god of Esculapius.

The Jews say to Pilate: We entreat your highness that he stand at thy tribunal and be heard. And Pilate, having called them, says: Tell me how I, being a procurator, can try a king? They say to him: We do not say that he is a king, but he himself says that he is. And Pilate, having called the runner, says to him: Let Jesus be brought in with respect. And the runner, going out and recognizing him, adored him, and took his cloak into his hand and spread it on the ground, and says to him: My Lord, walk on this and come in, for the

procurator calls thee. And the Jews, seeing what
the runner had done, cried out against Pilate, saying: Why hast thou ordered him to come in by a
runner, and not by a crier? for assuredly the runner, when he saw him, adored him, and spread his
doublet on the ground and made him walk like a
king.

And Pilate, having called the runner, says to
him: Why hast thou done this, and spread out thy
cloak upon the earth and made Jesus walk upon
it? The runner says to him: My lord procurator,
when thou didst send me to Jerusalem to Alexander, I saw him sitting upon an ass, and the sons
of the Hebrews held branches in their hands and
shouted; and others spread their clothes under
him, saying: Save now, thou who art in the
highest; blessed is he that cometh in the name of
the Lord.

The Jews cry out and say to the runner: The
sons of the Hebrews shouted in Hebrew; whence,
then, hast thou the Greek? The runner says to
them: I asked one of the Jews, and said: What
is it they are shouting in Hebrew? And he interpreted it for me. Pilate says to them: And
what did they shout in Hebrew? The Jews say
to him: *Hosanna membrome baruchamma adonai.*
Pilate says to them: And this hosanna, etc., how is

it interpreted? The Jews say to him: Save now in the highest; blessed is he that cometh in the name of the Lord. Pilate says to them: If you bear witness to the words spoken by the children, in what has the runner done wrong? And they were silent. And the procurator says to the runner: Go out and bring him in what way thou wilt. And the runner, going out, did in the same manner as before, and says to Jesus: My Lord, come in; the procurator calleth thee.

And Jesus, going in, and the standard-bearers holding their standards, the tops of the standards bent down, and adored Jesus. And the Jews, seeing the bearing of the standards how they were bent down and adored Jesus, cried out vehemently against the standard-bearers. And Pilate says to the Jews: Do you not wonder how the tops of the standards were bent down and adored Jesus? The Jews say to Pilate: We saw how the standard-bearers bent them down and adored him. And the procurator, having called the standard-bearers, says to them: Why have you done this? They say to Pilate: We are Greeks and temple-slaves, and how could we adore him? and assuredly, as we were holding them up, the tops bent down of their own accord and adored him.

Pilate says to the rulers of the synagogue and

the elders of the people: Do you choose for yourselves men strong and powerful, and let them hold up the standards, and let us see whether they will bend down with them. And the elders of the Jews picked out twelve men powerful and strong, and made them hold up the standards six by six; and they were placed in front of the procurator's tribunal. And Pilate says to the runner: Take him outside of the Pretorium, and bring him in again in whatever way may please thee. And Jesus and the runner went out of the Pretorium. And Pilate, summoning those who had formerly held up the standards, says to them: I have sworn by the health of Cæsar, that if the standards do not bend down when Jesus comes in, I will cut off your heads. And the procurator ordered Jesus to come in the second time. And the runner did in the same manner as before, and made many entreaties to Jesus to walk on his cloak. And he walked on it and went in. And as he went in the standards were again bent down and adored Jesus.

CHAP. 2.—And Pilate, seing this, was afraid, and sought to go away from the tribunal; but when he was still thinking of going away, his wife sent to him, saying: Have nothing to do with this just man, for many things have I suffered on his ac-

count this night. And Pilate, summoning the
Jews, says to them: You know that my wife is a
worshiper of God, and prefers to adhere to the
Jewish religion along with you. They say to him:
Yes, we know. Pilate says to them: Behold, my
wife·has sent to me, saying, Have nothing to do
with this just man, for many things have I suffered
on account of him this night. And the Jews answering, say unto Pilate: Did we not tell thee that
he was a sorcerer? behold, he has sent a dream to
thy wife.

And Pilate, having summoned Jesus, says to him:
What do these witness against thee? Sayest
thou nothing? And Jesus said: Unless they had
the power, they would say nothing; for every one
has the power of his own mouth to speak both
good and evil. They shall see to it.

And the elders of the Jews answered, and said
to Jesus: What shall we see? first, that thou wast
born of fornication; secondly, that thy birth in
Bethlehem was the cause of the murder of the infants; thirdly, that thy father Joseph and thy
mother Mary fled into Egypt because they had no
confidence in the people.

Some of the bystanders, pious men of the Jews,
say: We deny that he was born of fornication; for
we know that Joseph espoused Mary, and he was

not born of fornication. Pilate says to the Jews who said he was of fornication: This story of yours is not true, because they were betrothed, as also these fellow-countrymen of yours say. Annas and Caiaphas say to Pilate: All the multitude of us cry out that he was born of fornication, and are not believed; these are proselytes and his disciples. And Pilate, calling Annas and Caiaphas, says to them: What are proselytes? They say to him: They are by birth children of the Greeks, and have now become Jews. And those that said that he was not born of fornication, viz: Lazarus, Asterius, Antonius, James, Amnes, Zeras, Samuel, Isaac, Phinees, Crispus, Agrippas and Judas, say: We are not proselytes, but are children of the Jews, and speak the truth; for we were present at the betrothal of Joseph and Mary.

And Pilate, calling these twelve men who said that he was not born of fornication, says to them: I adjure you, by the health of Cæsar, to tell me whether it be true that you say, that he was not born of fornication. They say to Pilate: We have a law against taking oaths, because it is a sin; but they will swear by the health of Cæsar that it is not as we have said, and we are liable to death. Pilate says to Annas and Caiaphas: Have you nothing to answer to this? Annas and Caiaphas say to Pilate: These twelve are believed when they say that he was not born of fornication; all the multitude of us cry out that he was born of fornication, and that he is a sorcerer; and he says that he is the Son of God and a king, and we are not believed.

And Pilate orders all the multitude to go out, except the twelve men who said that he was not born of fornication, and he ordered Jesus to be separated from them. And Pilate says to them: For what reason do they wish to put him to death? They say to him: They are angry because he cures on the Sabbath. Pilate says: For a good work do they wish to put him to death? They say to him: Yes.

CHAP. 3.—And Pilate, filled with rage, went outside of the Pretorium and said to them: I take the sun to witness that I find no fault in this man. The Jews answered and said to the procurator: Unless this man were an evil-doer, we should not have delivered him to thee. And Pilate said: Do you take him and judge him according to your law. The Jews said to Pilate: It is not lawful for us to put any one to death. Pilate said: Has God said that you are not to put to death, but that I am?

And Pilate went again into the Pretorium and
spoke to Jesus privately, and said to him: Art
thou the king of the Jews? Jesus answered
Pilate: Dost thou say this of thyself, or have others
said it to thee of me? Pilate answered Jesus: Am
I also a Jew? Thy nation and the chief priests
have given thee up to me. What hast thou done?
Jesus answered: My kingdom is not of this world;
for if my kingdom were of this world, my servants would fight in order that I should not be
given up to the Jews: but now my kingdom is
not from thence. Pilate said to him: Art thou,
then, a king? Jesus answered him: Thou sayest
that I am a king. Because for this have I been
born, and I have come, in order that every one
who is of the truth might hear my voice. Pilate
says to him: What is truth? Jesus says to him:
Truth is from heaven. Pilate says: Is truth not
upon earth? Jesus says to Pilate: Thou seest how
those who speak the truth are judged by those that
have the power upon earth.

CHAP. 4.—And leaving Jesus within the Pretorium, Pilate went out to the Jews and said to
them: I find no fault in him. The Jews say to
him: He said, I can destroy this temple, and in
three days build it. Pilate says: What temple?

The Jews say: The one that Solomon built in forty-six years, and this man speaks of pulling it down and building it in three days. Pilate says to them: I am innocent of the blood of this just man. See you to it. The Jews say: His blood be upon us and upon our children.

And Pilate, having summoned the elders and priests and Levites, said to them privately: Do not act thus, because no charge that you bring against him is worthy of death; for your charge is about curing and Sabbath profanation. The elders and the priests and the Levites say: If any one speak evil against Cæsar, is he worthy of death or not? Pilate says: He is worthy of death. The Jews say to Pilate: If any one speak evil against Cæsar, he is worthy of death; but this man has spoken evil against God.

And the procurator ordered the Jews to go outside of the Pretorium; and, summoning Jesus, he says to him: What shall I do to thee? Jesus says to Pilate: As it has been given to thee. Pilate says: How given? Jesus says: Moses and the prophets have proclaimed beforehand of my death and resurrection. And the Jews, noticing this and hearing it, say to Pilate: What more wilt thou hear of this blasphemy? Pilate says to the Jews: If these words be blasphemous, do you take him for the blasphemy, and lead him away to your synagogue and judge him according to your law. The Jews say to Pilate: Our law bears that a man who wrongs his fellow-men is worthy to receive forty save one: but he that blasphemeth God is to be stoned with stones.

Pilate says to them: Do you take him and punish him in whatever way you please. The Jews say to Pilate: We wish that he be crucified. Pilate says: He is not deserving of crucifixion.

And the procurator, looking round upon the crowds of the Jews standing by, sees many of the Jews weeping, and says: All the multitude do not wish him to die. The elders of the Jews say: For this reason all the multitude of us have come, that he should die. Pilate says to the Jews: Why should he die? The Jews say: Because he called himself the Son of God and King.

CHAP. 5.—And one Nicodemus, a Jew, stood before the procurator and said: I beseech your honor let me say a few words. Pilate says: Say on. Nicodemus says: I said to the elders and the priests and Levites, and to all the multitude of the Jews in the synagogue, What do you seek to do with this man? This man does many miracles and strange· things, which no one has done or will do.

Let him go, and do not wish any evil against him.
If the miracles which he does are of God, they
will stand; but if of man, they will come to
nothing. For assuredly Moses, being sent by God
into Egypt, did many miracles, which the Lord
commanded him to do before Pharaoh, king of
Egypt. And there were Jannes and Jambres,
servants of Pharaoh, and they also did not a few
of the miracles which Moses did; and the
Egyptians took them to be gods—this Jannes and
Jambres. But, since the miracles which they did
were not of God, both they and those who believed
in them were destroyed. And now release this
man, for he is not deserving of death.

The Jews say to Nicodemus: Thou hast become
his disciple, and therefore thou defendest him.
Nicodemus says to them: Perhaps, too, the procurator has become his disciple, because he defends
him. Has the emperor not appointed him to this
place of dignity? And the Jews were vehemently
enraged, and gnashed their teeth against Nicodemus. Pilate says to them: Why do you gnash
your teeth against him when you hear the truth?
The Jews say to Nicodemus: Mayst thou receive
his truth and his portion. Nicodemus says: Amen,
amen; may I receive it, as you have said.

8

CHAP. 6.—One of the Jews, stepping up, asked leave of the procurator to say a word. The procurator says: If thou wishest to say anything, say. on. And the Jew said: Thirty-eight years I lay in my bed in great agony. And when Jesus came, many demoniacs and many lying ill of various diseases were cured by him. And when Jesus saw me he had compassion on me, and said to me: Take up thy couch and walk. And I took up my couch and walked. The Jews say to Pilate: Ask him on what day it was when he was cured. He that had been cured says: On a Sabbath. The Jews say: Is not this the very thing we said, that on a Sabbath he cures and casts out demons?

And another Jew stepped up and said: I was born blind; I heard sounds, but saw not a face. And as Jesus passed by I cried out with a loud voice, Pity me, O son of David. And he pitied me and put his hands upon my eyes, and I instantly received my sight. And another Jew stepped up and said: I was crooked, and he straightened me with a word. And another said: I was a leper, and he cured me with a word.

CHAP. 7.—And a woman cried out from a distance and said: I had an issue of blood, and I touched the hem of his garment, and the issue of blood, which I had had for twelve years, was stopped. The Jews say: We have a law that a woman's evidence is not to be received.

CHAP. 8.—And others, a multitude both of men and women, cried out, saying: This man is a prophet, and the demons are subject to him. Pilate says to them who said that the demons were subject to him: Why, then, were not your teachers also subject to him? They say to Pilate: We do not know. And others said: He raised Lazarus from the tomb after he had been dead four days. And the procurator trembled, and said to all the multitude of the Jews: Why do you wish to pour out innocent blood?

CHAP. 9.—And, having summoned Nicodemus and the twelve men that said he was not born of fornication, he says to them: What shall I do, because there is an insurrection among the people? They say to him: We know not; let them see to it. Again Pilate, having summoned all the multitude of the Jews, says: You know that it is customary, at the feast of unleavened bread, to release one prisoner to you. I have one condemned pris· oner in the prison, a murderer named Barabbas, and this man standing in your presence, Jesus, in whom I find no fault. Which of them do you

wish me to release to you? And they cry out:
Barabbas. Pilate says: What, then, shall we do
to Jesus, who is called Christ? The Jews say:
Let him be crucified. And others said: Thou art
no friend of Cæsar's if thou release this man, be-
cause he called himself the Son of God and King.
You wish this man, then, to be a king, and not
Cæsar?

And Pilate, in a rage, says to the Jews: Always
has your nation been rebellious, and you always
speak against your benefactors. The Jews say:
What benefactors? He says to them: Your God led
you out of the land of Egypt from bitter slavery,
and brought you safe through the sea as through
dry land, and in the desert fed you with manna
and gave you quails, and quenched your thirst
with water from a rock, and gave you a law; and
in all these things you provoked your God to
anger, and sought a molten calf. And you exasperated your God, and he sought to slay you. And
Moses prayed for you, and you were not put to
death. And now you charge me with hating the
emperor.

And, rising up from the tribunal, he sought to
go out. And the Jews cry out and say: We know
that Cæsar is king, and not Jesus. For assuredly
the magi brought gifts to him as to a king. And

when Herod heard from the magi that a king had been born, he sought to slay him; and his father, Joseph, knowing this, took him and his mother, and they fled into Egypt. And Herod, hearing of it, destroyed the children of the Hebrews that had been born in Bethlehem.

And when Pilate heard these words he was afraid; and, ordering the crowd to keep silence, because they were crying out, he says to them: So this is he whom Herod sought? The Jews say: Yes, it is he. And, taking water, Pilate washed his hands in the face of the sun, saying: I am innocent of the blood of this just man; see you to it. Again the Jews cry out: His blood be upon us and upon our children.

Then Pilate ordered the curtain of the tribunal where he was sitting to be drawn, and says to Jesus: Thy nation has charged thee with being a king. On this account, I sentence thee first to be scourged, according to the enactment of venerable kings, and then to be fastened on the cross in the garden where thou wast seized. And let Dysmas and Gestas, the two malefactors, be crucified with thee.

CHAP. 10.—And Jesus went forth out of the Pretorium, and the malefactors with him. And when

they came to the place they stripped him of his
clothes and girded him with a towel, and put a
crown of thorns on him round his head. And they
crucified him; and at the same time, also, they
hung up the two malefactors along with him. And
Jesus said: Father, forgive them, for they know
not what they do. And the soldiers parted his
clothes among them; and the people stood looking
at him. And the chief priests and the rulers with
them mocked him, saying: He saved others; let
him save himself. If he be the Son of God, let
him come down from the cross. And the soldiers
made sport of him, coming near and offering him
vinegar mixed with gall, and said: Thou art the
king of the Jews; save thyself.

And Pilate, after the sentence, ordered the
charge against him to be inscribed as a superscrip-
tion in Greek and Latin and Hebrew, according
to what the Jews had said: He is king of the
Jews.

And one of the malefactors hanging up spoke to
him, saying: If thou be the Christ, save thyself
and us. And Dysmas answering reproved him,
saying: Dost thou not fear God, because thou art
in the same condemnation? And we, indeed,
justly, for we receive the fit punishment of our
deeds; but this man has done no evil. And he

said to Jesus: Remember me, Lord, in thy kingdom. And Jesus said to him: Amen, amen; I say to thee, To-day shalt thou be with me in Paradise.

CHAP. 11.—And it was about the sixth hour, and there was darkness over the earth until the ninth hour, the sun being darkened; and the curtain of the temple was split in the middle. And, crying out with a loud voice, Jesus said: Father, *baddach ephkid ruel*, which is, interpreted, Into thy hands I commit my spirit. And, having said this, he gave up the ghost. And the centurion, seeing what had happened, glorified God and said: This was a just man. And all the crowds that were present at this spectacle, when they saw what had happened, beat their breasts and went away.

And the centurion reported what had happened to the procurator. And when the procurator and his wife heard it they were exceedingly grieved, and neither ate nor drank that day. And Pilate sent for the Jews and said to them: Have you seen what has happened? And they say: There has been an eclipse of the sun in the usual way.

And his acquaintances were standing at a distance, and the women who came with him from Galilee, seeing these things. And a man named

Joseph, a councillor from the city of Arimathea, who also waited for the kingdom of God, went to Pilate and begged the body of Jesus. And he took it down and wrapped it in a clean linen, and placed it in a tomb hewn out of the rock, in which no one had ever lain.

CHAP. 12.—And the Jews, hearing that Joseph had begged the body of Jesus, sought him and the twelve who said that Jesus was not born of fornication, and Nicodemus and many others who had stepped up before Pilate and declared his good works. And of all these that were hid Nicodemus alone was seen by them, because he was a ruler of the Jews. And Nicodemus says to them: How have you come into the synagogue? The Jews say to him: How hast thou come into the synagogue? for thou art a confederate of his, and his portion is with thee in the world to come. Nicodemus says: Amen, amen. And likewise Joseph also stepped out and said to them: Why are you angry against me because I begged the body of Jesus? Behold, I have put him in my new tomb, wrapping him in clean linen; and I have rolled a stone to the door of the tomb. And you have acted not well against the just man, because you have not repented of crucifying him, but also have pierced him with a spear. And the Jews seized Joseph and ordered him to be secured until the first day of the week, and said to him: Know that the time does not allow us to do anything against thee, because the Sabbath is dawning; and know that thou shalt not be deemed worthy of burial, but we shall give thy flesh to the birds of the air. Joseph says to them: These are the words of the arrogant Goliath, who reproached the living God and holy David. For God has said by the prophet, Vengeance is mine, and I will repay, saith the Lord. And now he that is uncircumcised in flesh, but circumcised in heart, has taken water and washed his hands in the face of the sun, saying, I am innocent of the blood of this just man; see ye to it. And you answered and said to Pilate, His blood be upon us and upon our children. And now I am afraid, lest the wrath of God come upon you and upon your children, as you have said. And the Jews, hearing these words, were embittered in their souls, and seized Joseph and locked him into a room where there was no window; and guards were stationed at the door, and they sealed the door where Joseph was locked in.

And on the Sabbath the rulers of the synagogue and the priests and the Levites made a decree that

all should be found in the synagogue on the first
day of the week. And, rising up early, all the
multitude in the synagogue consulted by what
death they should slay him. And when the Sanhedrim was sitting, they ordered him to be brought
with much indignity. And, having opened the
door, they found him not, And all the people
were surprised and struck with dismay, because
they found the seals unbroken, and because Caiaphas had the key. And they no longer dared to
lay hands upon those who had spoken before
Pilate in Jesus' behalf.

CHAP. 13.—And while they were still sitting in
the synagogue and wondering about Joseph, there
come some of the guard whom the Jews had
begged of Pilate to guard the tomb of Jesus, that
his disciples might not come and steal him. And
they reported to the rulers of the synagogue, and
the priests and Levites, what had happened: how
there had been a great earthquake; and we saw an
angel coming down from heaven, and he rolled
away the stone from the mouth of the tomb and
sat upon it; and he shone like snow and like
lightning. And we were very much afraid, and
lay like dead men; and we heard the voice of the
angel, saying to the women who remained beside

the tomb, Be not afraid, for I know that you seek Jesus, who was crucified. He is not here. He has risen, as he said. Come, see the place where the Lord lay; and go quickly and tell his disciples that he is risen from the dead, and is in Galilee.

The Jews say: To what woman did he speak? The men of the guard say: We do not know who they were. The Jews say: At what time was this? The men of the guard say: At midnight. The Jews say: And wherefore did you not lay hold of them? The men of the guard say: We were like dead men from fear, not expecting to see the light of day, and how could we lay hold of them? The Jews say: As the Lord liveth, we do not believe you. The men of the guard say to the Jews: You have seen so great miracles in the case of this man, and have not believed; and how can you believe us? And assuredly you have done well to swear that the Lord liveth, for indeed he does live. Again the men of the guard say: We have heard that you have locked up the man that begged the body of Jesus, and put a seal on the door; and that you have opened it and not found him. Do you, then, give us the man whom you were guarding, and we shall give you Jesus. The Jews say: Joseph has gone away to his own city. The men of the guard say to the Jews: And Jesus has risen, as we heard from the angel, and is in Galilee.

And when the Jews heard these words they were very much afraid, and said: We must take care lest this story be heard, and all incline to Jesus. And the Jews called a council, and paid down a considerable money and gave it to the soldiers, saying: Say, while he slept, his disciples came by night and stole him; and if this come to the ears of the procurator we shall persuade him and keep you out of trouble. And they took it, and said as they had been instructed.

CHAP. 14.—And Phinees, a priest, and Adas, a teacher, and Haggai, a Levite, came down from Galilee to Jerusalem, and said to the rulers of the synagogue, and the priests and the Levites: We saw Jesus and his disciples sitting on the mountain called Mamilch; and he said to his disciples, Go into all the world and preach to every creature: he that believeth and is baptized shall be saved, and he that believeth not shall be condemned. And these signs shall attend those who have believed: in my name they shall cast out demons, speak new tongues, take up serpents; and if they drink any deadly thing it shall by no means hurt them; they shall lay hands on the sick, and they shall be well. And while Jesus was speaking to his disciples we saw him taken up into heaven.

The elders and priests and Levites say: Give glory to the God of Israel, and confess to him whether you have heard and seen those things, of which you have given us an account. And those who had given the account said: As the Lord liveth, the God of our fathers Abraham, Isaac and Jacob, we heard these things, and saw him taken up into heaven. The elders and the priests and the Levites say to them: Have you come to give us this announcement, or to offer prayer to God? And they say: To offer prayer to God. The elders and the chief priests and the Levites say to them: If you have come to offer prayer to God why, then, have you told these idle tales in the presence of all the people? Says Phinees, the priest, and Adas, the teacher, and Haggai, the Levite, to the rulers of the synagagues, and the priests and the Levites: If what we have said and seen be sinful, behold, we are before you; do to us as seems good in your eyes. And they took the law and made them swear upon it not to give any more an account of these matters to any one. And they gave them to eat and drink and sent them out of the city, having given them also money, and three men with them; and they sent them away to Galilee.

And these men, having gone into Galilee, the chief priests and the rulers of the synagogue, and the elders came together in the synagogue and locked the door, and lamented with great lamentation, saying: Is this a miracle that has happened in Israel? And Annas and Caiaphas said: Why are you so much moved? Why do you weep? Do you not know that his disciples have given a sum of gold to the guards of the tomb, and have instructed them to say that an angel came down and rolled away the stone from the door of the tomb? And the priests and elders said: Be it that his disciples have stolen his body; how is it that the life has come into his body, and that he is going about in Galilee? And they, being unable to give an answer to these things, said, after great hesitation: It is not lawful for us to believe the uncircumcised.

CHAP. 15.—And Nicodemus stood up, and stood before the Sanhedrim, saying: You say well; you are not ignorant, you people of the Lord, of these men that come down from Galilee, that they fear God, and are men of substance, haters of covetousness, men of peace; and they have declared with an oath, We saw Jesus upon the mountain Mamilch with his disciples, and he taught what we heard from him, and we saw him taken up into heaven. And no one asked them in what form he went up. For assuredly, as the book of the Holy Scriptures taught us, Helias also was taken up into heaven, and Elissæus cried out with a loud voice, and Helias threw his sheepskin upon Elissæus, and Elissæus threw his sheepskin upon the Jordan, and crossed and came into Jericho. And the children of the prophets met him and said, O Elissæus, where is thy master Helias? And he said, He has been taken up into heaven. And they said to Elissæus, Has not a spirit seized him, and thrown him upon one of the mountains? But let us take our servants with us and seek him. And they persuaded Elissæus, and he went away with them. And they sought him three days, and did not find him; and they knew that he had been taken up. And now listen to me, and let us send into every district of Israel and see lest, perchance, Christ has been taken up by a spirit and thrown upon one of the mountains. And this proposal pleased all. And they sent into every district of Israel and sought Jesus, and did not find him; but they found Joseph in Arimathea, and no one dared to lay hands on him.

And they reported to the elders and the priests
and the Levites: We have gone round to every district of Israel, and have not found Jesus; but
Joseph we have found in Arimathea. And hearing
about Joseph they were glad, and gave glory to the
God of Israel. And the rulers of the synagogue,
and the priests and the Levites, having held a
council as to the manner in which they should
meet with Joseph, took a piece of paper and wrote
to Joseph as follows:

Peace to thee! We know that we have sinned
against God, and against thee; and we have prayed
to the God of Israel that thou shouldst deign to
come to thy fathers and to thy children, because
we all have been grieved. For, having opened the
door, we did not find thee. And we know that we
have counseled evil counsel against thee; but the
Lord has defended thee, and the Lord himself has
scattered to the winds our counsel against thee, O
honorable father Joseph.

And they chose from all Israel seven men, friends
of Joseph, whom, also, Joseph himself was acquainted with; and the rulers of the synagogue,
and the priests and the Levites say to them: Take
notice: if, after receiving our letter he read it,
know that he will come with you to us. But if he do
not read it, know that he is ill-disposed towards us.

And, having saluted him in peace, return to us. And having blessed the men, they dismissed them. And the men came to Joseph and did reverence to him, and said to him: Peace to thee! And he said: Peace to you and to all the people of Israel! And they gave him the roll of the letter. And Joseph, having received it, read the letter and rolled it up, and blessed God and said: Blessed be the Lord God, who has delivered Israel, that they should not shed innocent blood; and blessed be the Lord, who sent out his angel and covered me under his wings. And he set a table for them; and they ate and drank and slept there.

And they rose up early and prayed. And Joseph saddled his ass and set out with the men; and they came to the holy city Jerusalem. And all the people met Joseph and cried out: Peace to thee in thy coming in! And he said to all the people: Peace to you! and he kissed them. And the people prayed with Joseph, and they were astonished at the sight of him. And Nicodemus received him into his house and made a great feast, and called Annas and Caiaphas and the elders and the priests and the Levites to his house. And they rejoiced, eating and drinking with Joseph; and, after singing hymns, each proceeded to his

9

own house. But Joseph remained in the house of Nicodemus.

And on the following day, which was the preparation, the rulers of the synagogue and the priests and the Levites went early to the house of Nicodemus; and Nicodemus met them and said: Peace to you! And they said: Peace to thee and to Joseph, and to all thy house and to all the house of Joseph! And he brought them into his house. And all the Sanhedrim sat down, and Joseph sat down between Annas and Caiaphas; and no one dared to say a word to him. And Joseph said: Why have you called me? And they signaled to Nicodemus to speak to Joseph. And Nicodemus, opening his mouth, said to Joseph: Father, thou knowest that the honorable teachers and the priests and the Levites seek to learn a word from thee. And Joseph said: Ask. And Annas and Caiaphas, having taken the law, made Joseph swear, saying: Give glory to the God of Israel, and give him confession; for Achar, being made to swear by the prophet Jesus, did not forswear himself, but declared unto him all, and did not hide a word from him. Do thou also, accordingly, not hide from us to the extent of a word. And Joseph said: I shall not hide from you one word. And they said to him: With grief were we grieved be-

cause thou didst beg the body of Jesus and wrap
it in clean linen and lay it in a tomb. And on
account of this we secured thee in a room where there
was no window; and we put locks and seals upon
the doors, and guards kept watching. where thou
wast locked in. And on the first day of the week
we opened and found thee not, and were grieved
exceedingly; and astonishment fell upon all the
people of the Lord until yesterday. And now re-
late to us what has happened to thee.

And Joseph said: On the preparation, about the
tenth hour, you locked me up, and I remained all
the Sabbath. And at midnight, as I was standing
and praying, the room where you locked me in
was hung up by the four corners, and I saw a light
like lightning into my eyes. And I was afraid and
fell to the ground. And some one took me by the
hand and removed me from the place where I had
fallen; and moisture of water was poured from my
head even to my feet, and a smell of perfumes came
about my nostrils. And he wiped my face and
kissed me, and said to me, Fear not, Joseph; open
thine eyes and see who it is that speaks to thee.
And, looking up, I saw Jesus. And I trembled,
and thought it was a phantom; and I said the
commandments, and he said them with me. Even
so you are not ignorant that a phantom, if it meet

anybody and hear the commandments, takes to
flight. And seeing that he said them with me, I
said to him, Rabbi Helias. And he said to me, I
am not Helias. And I said to him, Who art thou,
my lord? And he said to me, I am Jesus, whose
body thou didst beg from Pilate; and thou didst
clothe me with clean linen, and didst put a napkin
on my face, and didst lay me in thy new tomb,
and didst roll a great stone to the door of the
tomb. And I said to him that was speaking to
me, Show me the place where I laid thee. And he
carried me away and showed me the place where I
laid him; and the linen cloth was lying in it, and
the napkin for his face. And I knew that it was
Jesus. And he took me by the hand and placed
me, though the doors were locked, in the middle
of my house, and led me away to my bed and said
to me, Peace to thee! And he kissed me and said
to me, For forty days go not forth out of thy house;
for, behold, I go to my brethren in Galilee.

CHAP. 16.—And the rulers of the synagogue, and
the priests and the Levites, when they heard these
words from Joseph, became as dead, and fell to
the ground, and fasted until the ninth hour. And
Nicodemus, along with Joseph, exhorted Annas
and Caiaphas, the priests and the Levites, saying:

Rise up and stand upon your feet, and taste bread and strengthen your souls, because to-morrow is the Sabbath of the Lord. And they rose up and prayed to God, and ate and drank, and departed every man to his own house.

And on the Sabbath our teachers and the priests and Levites sat questioning each other and saying: What is this wrath that has come upon us? for we know his father and mother. Levi, a teacher, says: I know that his parents fear God, and do not withdraw themselves from the prayers, and give the tithes thrice a year. And when Jesus was born his parents brought him to this place and gave sacrifices and burnt offerings to God. And when the great teacher, Symeon, took him into his arms, he said, Now thou sendest away thy servant, Lord, according to thy word, in peace; for mine eyes have seen thy salvation, which thou hast prepared before the face of all the peoples; a light for the revelation of the Gentiles, and the glory of thy people Israel. And Symeon blessed them, and said to Mary his mother, I give thee good news about this child. And Mary said, It is well, my lord. And Symeon said to her, It is well; behold, he lies for the fall and the rising again of many in Israel and for a sign spoken against; and of thee thyself a

sword shall go through the soul, in order that the
reasoning of many hearts may be revealed.

They say to the teacher Levi: How knowest
thou these things? Levi says to them: Do you not
know that from him I learned the law? The Sanhedrim say to him: We wish to see thy father.
And they sent for his father. And they asked him,
and he said to them: Why have you not believed
my son? The blessed and just Symeon himself
taught him the law. The Sanhedrim says to
Rabbi Levi: Is the word that you have said
true?. And he said: It is true. And the rulers
of the synagogue, and the priests and the
Levites said to themselves: Come, let us send
into Galilee to the three men that came and
told about his teaching and his taking up, and
let them tell us how they saw him taken up. And
this saying pleased all. And they sent away the
three men who had already gone away into Galilee
with them; and they say to them: Say to Rabbi
Adas and Rabbi Phinees and Rabbi Haggai, Peace
to you and all who are with you! A great inquiry
having taken place in the Sanhedrim, we have been
sent to you to call you to this holy place, Jerusalem.

And the men set out into Galilee and found them
sitting and considering the law; and they saluted

them in peace. And the men who were in Galilee said to those who had come to them: Peace upon all Israel! And they said: Peace to you! And they again said to them: Why have you come? And those who had been sent said: The Sanhedrim call you to the holy city Jerusalem. And when the men heard that they were sought by the Sanhedrim they prayed to God, and reclined with the men and ate and drank, and rose up and set out in peace to Jerusalem.

And on the following day the Sanhedrim sat in the synagogue, and asked them, saying: Did'you really see Jesus sitting on the mountain Mamilch teaching his eleven disciples, and did you see him taken up? And the men answered them and said: As we saw him taken up, so also we said.

Annas says: Take them away from one another and let us see whether their account agrees. And they took them away from one another. And first they call Adas and say to him: How didst thou see Jesus taken up? Adas says: While he was yet sitting on the mountain Mamilch and teaching his disciples, we saw a cloud overshadowing both him and his disciples. And the cloud took him up into heaven, and his disciples lay upon their face upon the earth. And they call Phinees the priest, and ask him also, saying: How didst thou see

Jesus taken up? And he spoke in like manner. And they again asked Haggai, and he spoke in like manner. And the Sanhedrim said: The law of Moses holds: At the mouth of two or three every word shall be established. But them, a teacher, says: It is written in the law, And Enoch walked with God, and is not, because God took him. Jaïrus, a teacher, said: And the death of holy Moses we have heard of, and have not seen it; for it is written in the law of the Lord, And Moses died from the mouth of the Lord, and no man knoweth of his sepulchre unto this day. And Rabbi Levi said: Why did Rabbi Symeon say, when he saw Jesus, "Behold, he lies for the fall and rising again of many in Israel, and for a sign spoken against?" And Rabbi Isaac said: It is written in the law, Behold, I send my messenger before thy face, who shall go before thee to keep thee in every good way, because my name has been called upon him.

Then Annas and Caiaphas said: Rightly have you said what is written in the law of Moses, that no one saw the death of Enoch, and no one has named the death of Moses; but Jesus was tried before Pilate, and we saw him receiving blows and spittings on his face, and the soldiers put about him a crown of thorns, and he was scourged and

received sentence from Pilate, and was crucified
upon the Cranium, and two robbers with him; and
they gave him to drink vinegar with gall, and
Longinus the soldier pierced his side with a spear;
and Joseph, our honorable father, begged his
body, and he says he is risen; and as the three
teachers say, We saw him taken up into heaven;
and Rabbi Levi has given evidence of what was
said by Rabbi Symeon, and that he said, Behold,
he lies for the fall [and] rising again of many in
Israel, and for a sign spoken against. And all
the teachers said to all the people of the Lord: If
this was from the Lord, and is wonderful in your
eyes, knowing you shall know, O house of Jacob,
that it is written, Cursed is every one that hangeth
upon a tree. And another scripture teaches: The
gods which have not made the heaven and the
earth shall be destroyed. And the priests and the
Levites said to each other: If his memorial be
until the [year] that is called Jobel, know that it
shall endure forever, and he hath raised for himself a new people. Then the rulers of the synagogue, and the priests and the Levites, announced
to all Israel, saying: Cursed is that man who shall
worship the work of man's hand, and cursed is the
man who shall worship the creatures more than

the Creator. And all the people said, Amen, amen.

And all the people praised the Lord, and said: Blessed is the Lord, who hath given rest to his people Israel, according to all that he hath spoken; there hath not fallen one word of every good word of his that he spoke to Moses his servant. May the Lord our God be with us, as he was with our fathers; let him not destroy us. And let him not destroy us, that we may incline our hearts to him, that we may walk in all his ways, that we may keep his commandments and his judgments which he commanded to our fathers. And the Lord shall be for a king over all the earth in that day; and there shall be one Lord, and his name one. The Lord is our king; he shall save us. There is none like thee, O Lord. Great art thou, O Lord, and great is thy name. By thy power heal us, O Lord, and we shall be healed; save us, O Lord, and we shall be saved, because we are thy lot and heritage. And the Lord will not leave his people, for his great name's sake; for the Lord has begun to make us into his people.

And all, having sung praises, went away each man to his own house glorifying God; for his is the glory forever and ever. Amen.

THE ACTS OF PILATE.

SECOND GREEK FORM.

A narrative about the suffering of our Lord Jesus Christ, and his holy resurrection.

Written by a Jew, Æneas by name, and translated out of the Hebrew tongue into the Romaic language by Nicodemus, a Roman toparch.

After the dissolution of the kingdom of the Hebrews, four hundred years having run their course, and the Hebrews also coming at last under the kingdom of the Romans, and the king of the Romans appointing them a king; when Tiberius Cæsar at last swayed the Roman scepter, in the eighteenth year of his reign, he appointed as king in Judea, Herod, the son of the Herod who had formerly slaughtered the infants in Béthlehem, and he made Pilate procurator in Jerusalem; when Annas and Caiaphas held the high-priesthood of Jerusalem, Nicodemus, a Roman toparch, having summoned a Jew, Æneas by name, asked him to write an account of the things done in Jerusalem about Christ in the times of Annas and Caiaphas. The Jew accordingly did this, and delivered it to Nicodemus; and he, again, translated it from the Hebrew writing into the Romaic language. And the account is as follows:

CHAP. 1.—Our Lord Jesus Christ having wrought in Judea many and great and extraordinary miracles, and on account of this being hated by the Hebrews, while Pilate was procurator in Jerusalem, and Annas and Caiaphas high priests, there came of the Jews to the chief priests, Judas, Levi, Nephthalim, Alexander, Syrus, and many others, speaking against Christ. And these chief priests sent them away to say these things to Pilate also. And they went away, and said to him: A man walks about in this city whose father is called Joseph, and his mother Mary; and he calls himself king and Son of God; and being a Jew, he overturns the Scriptures, and does away with the Sabbath. Pilate then asked, in order to learn from them in what manner he did away with the Sabbath. And they answered, saying: He cures the sick on the Sabbath. Pilate says: If he makes the sick whole, he does no evil. They say to him: If he effected the cures properly, small would be the evil; but by using magic he does these things, and by having the demons on his side. Pilate says: To cure a person that is ill is not a diabolic work, but a grace from God.

The Hebrews said: We beseech your highness to summon him, in order that thou mayst make accu-. rate inquiry into what we say. Pilate therefore, throwing off his cloak, gave it to one of his officers, saying: Go away, and show this to Jesus, and say to him, Pilate the procurator calls thee to come before him. The officer accordingly went away, and finding Jesus, summoned him, having unfolded on the ground also Pilate's mantle, and urged him to walk upon it. And the Hebrews, seeing this, and being greatly enraged, came to Pilate, murmuring against him, how he had deemed Jesus worthy of so great an honor.

And he, having inquired of the officer who had been sent how he had done so, the officer answered: When thou didst send me to the Jew Alexander, I came upon Jesus entering the gate of the city, sitting upon an ass. And I saw that the Hebrews spread their garments in the way, and the ass walked upon the garments; and others cut branches, and they went forth to meet him, and cried out, Hosanna in the highest! Thus, therefore, it was necessary for me also to do. ·

The Jews, hearing these words, said to him: How didst thou, being a Roman, know what was said by the Hebrews? The officer answered: I asked one of the Hebrews, and he told me these things. Pilate said: What means Hosanna? The Jews said: Save us, O Lord. Pilate answered: Since you confess that your children said so, how now do you bring charges, and say against Jesus what you do say? The Jews were silent, and had nothing to answer.

Now, as Jesus was coming to Pilate, the soldiers of Pilate adored him. And others also were standing before Pilate holding standards. And as Jesus was coming, the standards also bowed down, and adored him. As Pilate, therefore, was wondering at what had happened, the Jews said to him: My lord, it was not the standards that adored Jesus, but the soldiers who were holding them carelessly.

Pilate says to the ruler of the synagogue: Choose twelve powerful men, and give them the standards, so that they may hold them firmly. And this having taken place, Pilate ordered the officer to take Jesus outside, and bring him in again. And as he was coming in, the standards again bowed down, and adored him. Pilate therefore wondered greatly. But the Jews said: He is a magician, and through that he does these things.

CHAP. 2.—Pilate says to Jesus: Hearest thou what these testify against thee, and answerest thou not? And Jesus answered and said: Every man has power to speak either good or bad, as he wishes; these also, therefore, having power, say what they wish.

The Jews said to him: What have we to say about thee? First, that thou wast begotten from sin; second, that on account of thee, when thou wast born, the infants were murdered; third, that thy father and thy mother fled into Egypt, because they had no confidence in the people.

To these the Jews who were there present, God-fearing men, answered and said: We say that his birth is not from sin; for we know that Joseph received into keeping his mother Mary, according to the practice of betrothal. Pilate said: Consequently you lie who say his birth is from sin. They say again to Pilate: All the people testify that he is a magician. The God-fearing Jews answered and said: We also were at the betrothal of his mother, and we are Jews, and know all of his daily life; but that he is a magician, that we do not know. And the Jews that thus said were these: Lazarus, Astharius, Antonius, James, Zaras, Samuel, Isaac, Phinees, Crispus, Dagrippus, Amese and Judas.

Pilate therefore says to them: By the life of Cæsar, I wish you to swear whether the birth of this man is without sin. They answered: Our law lays down that we are to swear not at all, because an oath is great sin. Notwithstanding, by the life of Cæsar we swear that his birth is without sin; and if we lie, order us all to be beheaded. And when they had thus spoken, the Jews that were bringing the charge answered Pilate, and said: And dost thou believe these twelve single Jews more than all the multitude and us, who know for certain that he is a magician and blasphemer, and that he names himself Son of God?

Then Pilate ordered them all to go forth out of the Pretorium except the said twelve alone. And when this had been done, Pilate says to them privately: As to this man, it appears that from envy and madness the Jews wish to murder him: for of one thing—that he does away with the Sabbath—they accuse him; but he then does a good work, because he cures the sick. For this, sentence of death is not upon the man. The twelve also say to him: Assuredly, my lord, it is so.

CHAP. 3.—Pilate therefore went outside in rage and anger, and says to Annas and Caiaphas, and to the crowd who brought Jesus: I take the sun to

witness that I find no fault in this man. The crowd
answered: If he were not a sorcerer, and a magician, and a blasphemer, we should not have brought
him to your highness. Pilate said: Try him yourselves; and since you have a law, do as your law
says. The Jews said: Our law permits to put no
man to death. Pilate says: If you are unwilling
to put him to death, how much more am I.

Then Pilate returned to the palace, and says to
Jesus: Tell me, art thou the king of the Jews?
Jesus answered: Dost thou say this, or have the
other Jews said this to thee, that thou mightst
question me? Pilate said: Thou dost not think I
am a Hebrew? I am not a Hebrew. Thy people
and the chief priests have delivered thee into my
hands; and tell me if thou art king of the Jews?
Jesus answered: My kingdom is not of this world;
for if my kingdom were in this world, my soldiers
would not be unconcerned at my being seized:
wherefore my kingdom is not in this world. Pilate
says: But art thou a king? Jesus said: Thou hast
said: for this was I born, to bear witness to the
truth; and if any one be a man of the truth, he
believes my word, and does it. Pilate says: What
is the truth? Jesus answered: The truth is from
the heavens. Pilate says: On earth, then, is there

10

no truth? Christ says: I am the truth; and how is the truth judged on earth by those that have earthly power!

Chap. 4.—Pilate therefore, leaving Christ alone, went outside, and says to the Jews: I find no fault in this man. The Jews answered: Let us tell your highness what he said. He said, I am able to destroy the temple of God, and in three days to build it. Pilate says: And what temple did he say that he was to destroy? The Hebrews say: The temple of Solomon, which Solomon built in forty-six years.

Pilate says privately to the chief priests and the scribes and the Pharisees: I entreat you, do nothing evil against this man; for if you do evil against him, you will do unjustly: for it is not just that such a man should die, who has done great good to many men. They said to Pilate: If, my lord, he who has dishonored Cæsar is worthy of death, how much more this [man] who dishonors God!

Then Pilate dismissed them, and they all went outside. Thereupon he says to Jesus: What dost thou wish that I shall do to thee? Jesus says to Pilate: Do to me as is determined. Pilate says: How is it determined? Jesus answered: Moses and the prophets wrote about me being crucified, and rising again. The Hebrew hearing [this], said to

Pilate: Why do you seek to hear a greater insult out of him against God? Pilate says: These words are not an insult against God, since they are written in the books of the prophets. The Hebrews said: Our Scripture says, If a man offend against a man, that is to say, if he insult him, he is worthy to receive forty strokes with a rod; but if any one insult God, to be stoned.

Then came a messenger from Procle, the wife of Pilate, to him; and the message said: Take care that thou do not agree that any evil should happen to Jesus the good man; because during this night I have seen fearful dreams on account of him. And Pilate spoke to the Hebrews, saying: If you hold as insult against God the words which you declare Jesus to have spoken, take and judge him yourselves according to your law. The Jews said to Pilate: We wish that you should crucify him. Pilate says: This is not good.

And Pilate, turning towards the people, saw many weeping, and said: To me it seems that it is not the wish of all the people that this man should die. The priests and the scribes say: We on this account have brought all the people, that thou mightst have full conviction that all wish his death. Pilate says: For what evil hath he done? The Hebrews said: He says that he is a king, and the Son of God.

Chap. 5.—A God-fearing Jew, therefore, Nicodemus by name, stood up in the midst, and said to
Pilate: I entreat your highness to permit me to
say a few words. Say on, said Pilate. Nicodemus
says: I, being present in the synagogue, said to the
priests, and the Levites, and the scribes, and the
people, What have you to say against this man?
This man does many miracles, such as man has
never yet done nor will do. Let him go, therefore;
and if indeed what he does be from God, it will
stand; but if from man, it will be destroyed. Just
as happened also when God sent Moses into Egypt,
and Pharaoh king of Egypt told him to do a miracle, and he did it. Then Pharaoh had also two
magicians, Jannes and Jambres; and they also did
miracles by the use of magic art, but not such as
Moses did. And the Egyptians held these magicians to be gods; but because they were not from
God, what they did was destroyed. This Jesus,
then, raised up Lazarus, and he is alive. On this
account I entreat thee, my lord, by no means to
allow this man to be put to death.

The Hebrews were enraged against Nicodemus,
and said: Mayst thou receive the truth of Jesus,
and have a portion with him. Nicodemus says:
Amen, amen; be it to me as you say.

CHAP. 6.—And when Nicodemus had thus spoken, another Hebrew rose up, and said to Pilate: I beg of thee, my lord Pilate, hear me also. Pilate answered: Say what thou wishest. The Hebrew says: I lay sick in bed thirty-eight years; and when he saw me he was grieved, and said to me, Rise, take up thy couch, and go into thine house. And while he was saying the word to me, I rose and walked about. The Hebrews say: Ask him on what day of the week this happened. He says: On Sabbath. The Jews said: And consequently we say truly, that he does not keep the Sabbath.

Another, again, standing in the midst, said: I was born blind; and as Jesus was going along the road, I cried to him, saying, Have mercy upon me, Lord, thou son of David. And he took clay, and anointed mine eyes; and straightway I received my sight. Another said: I was crooked; and seeing him, I cried, Have mercy upon me, O Lord. And he took me by the hand, and I was immediately raised. Another said: I was a leper, and he healed me merely by a word.

CHAP. 7.—There was found there also a woman named Veronica, and she said: Twelve years I was in an issue of blood, and I only touched the edge of his garment, and directly I was cured. The

Jews say: Our law does not admit the testimony of a woman.

CHAP. 8.—Other men cried: This man is a prophet, and the demons are afraid of him. Pilate says: And how were the demons not at all thus afraid of your parents also? They say: We do not know. Others, again, said: Lazarus, after having been four days in the tomb, he raised by a single word. Pilate therefore, hearing of the raising of Lazarus, was afraid, and said to the people: Why do you wish to shed the blood of a just man?

CHAP. 9.—Then he summoned Nicodemus and the twelve God-fearing Jews, and said to them: What do you say that I should do? because the people are in commotion. They say: We do not know: do as thou wilt; but what the people do, they do unjustly, in order to kill him. Pilate again went outside, and said to the people: You know that in the feasts of unleavened bread it is customary that I free on your account one of the criminals kept in custody. I have, then, one malefactor in the prison, a robber named Barabbas. I have also Jesus, who has never done any evil. Which of the two, then, do you wish that I release to you? The people answered: Release to us Barabbas. Pilate says: What, then, shall I do with Jesus? They say: Let him be crucified. Again, others of them cried out: If thou release Jesus thou art no friend of Cæsar, because he calls himself Son of God, and king. And if thou free him, he becomes a king, and will take Cæsar's kingdom.

Pilate, therefore, was enraged, and said: Always has your nation been devilish and unbelieving; and ever have you been adversaries to your benefactors. The Hebrews say: And who were our benefactors? Pilate says: God, who freed you out of the land of Pharaoh and brought you through the Red Sea as upon dry land, and fed you with quails, and gave you water to drink out of the dry rocks, and who gave you a law, which, denying God, you broke; and if Moses had not stood and entreated God, you would have perished by a bitter death. All these, then, you have forgotten. Thus, also, even now, you say that I do not at all love Cæsar, but hate him, and wish to plot against his kingdom.

And having thus spoken, Pilate rose up from the throne with anger, wishing to flee from them. The Jews therefore cried out, saying: We wish Cæsar to be king over us, not Jesus, because Jesus received gifts from the magi. And Herod also heard this—that there was going to be a king—and wished to put him to death, and for this purpose sent and put to death all the infants that were in Bethlehem. And on this account also his father, Joseph, and his mother fled from fear of him into Egypt.

So then, Pilate hearing [this], silenced all the people, and said: This, then, is the Jesus whom Herod then sought, that he might put him to death? They say to him: Yes. Pilate, therefore, having ascertained that he was of the jurisdiction of Herod, as being derived of the race of the Jews, sent Jesus to him. And Herod, seeing him, rejoiced greatly, because he had been long desiring to see him, hearing of the miracles which he did. He put on him, therefore, white garments. Then he began to question him. But Jesus did not give him an answer. And Herod, wishing to see also some miracle or other done by Jesus, and not seeing it, and also because he did not answer him a single word, sent him back again to Pilate. Pilate, seeing this, ordered his officers to bring water. Washing, then, his hands with the water, he said to the people: I am innocent of the blood of this good man. See you to it, that he is unjustly put to death, since neither I have found fault in him, nor Herod; for because of this he has sent him back again to me. The Jews say: His blood be upon us and upon our children.

Then Pilate sat down upon his throne to pass sentence. He gave order, therefore, and Jesus came before him. And they brought a crown of thorns and put it on his head, and a reed into his right hand. Then he passed sentence, and said to him: Thy nation says and testifies against thee that thou wishest to be a king. Therefore, I decree that they shall beat thee first with a rod forty strokes, as the laws of the kings decree, and that they shall mock thee; and finally that they shall crucify thee.

CHAP. 10.—The sentence to this effect, then, having been passed by Pilate, the Jews began to strike Jesus, some with rods, others with [their] hands, others with [their] feet; some also spat in his face. Immediately, therefore, they got ready the cross and gave it to him, and flew to take the road. And thus going along, bearing also the cross, he came as far as the gate of the city of Jerusalem. But as he, from the many blows and the weight of the cross, was unable to walk, the Jews, out of the eager desire they had to crucify him as quickly as possible, took the cross from him and gave it to a man that met them, Simon by name, who had also two sons, Alexander and Rufus. And he was from the city of Cyrene.

They gave the cross, then, to him, not because they pitied Jesus and wished to lighten him of the weight, but because they eagerly desired, as has been said, to put him to death more speedily.

Of his disciples, therefore, John followed him there. Then he came fleeing to the mother of God, and said to her: Where hast thou been, that thou hast not come to see what has happened? She answered: What is it that has happened? John says: Know that the Jews have laid hold of my Master, and are taking him away to crucify him. Hearing this, his mother cried out with a loud voice, saying: My son, my son, what evil, then, hast thou done that they are taking thee away to crucify thee? And she rose up as if blinded, and goes along the road weeping. And women followed her—Martha and Mary Magdalene and Salome and other virgins. And John also was with her. When, therefore, they came to the multitude of the crowd, the mother of God says to John: Where is my son? John says: Seest thou him bearing the crown of thorns, and having his hands bound? And the mother of God, hearing this and seeing him, fainted and fell backwards to the ground, and lay a considerable time. And the women, as many as followed her, stood round her and wept. And as soon as she revived and rose up, she cried out with a loud voice: My Lord, my son, where has the beauty of thy form sunk? how shall I endure to see thee suffering such things? And thus saying, she tore her face with her nails, and beat her breast. Where are they gone, said she, the good deeds which thou didst in Judea? What evil hast thou done to the Jews? The Jews, then, seeing her thus lamenting and crying, came and drove her from the road; but she would not flee, but remained, saying: Kill me first, ye lawless Jews.

Then they got safe to the place called Cranium, which was paved with stone; and there the Jews set up the cross. Then they stripped Jesus, and the soldiers took his garments and divided them among themselves; and they put on him a tattered robe of scarlet, and raised him and drew him up on the cross at the sixth hour of the day. After this they brought, also, two robbers, the one on his right, the other on his left.

Then the mother of God, standing and looking, cried out with a loud voice, saying: My son! my son! And Jesus, turning to her, and seeing John near her, and weeping with the rest of the women, said: Behold thy son! Then he says also to John: Behold thy mother! And she wept much, saying: For this I weep, my son, because thou sufferest unjustly, because the lawless Jews have delivered thee to a bitter death. Without thee, my son, what will become of me? How shall I live without thee? What sort of life shall I spend? Where are thy disciples, who boasted that they would die with thee? Where those healed by thee? How has no one been found to help thee? And, looking to the cross, she said: Bend down, O cross, that I may embrace and kiss my son, whom I suckled at these breasts after a strange manner, as not having known man. Bend down, O cross; I wish to throw my arms round my son. Bend down, O cross, that I may bid farewell to my son like a mother. The Jews, hearing these words, came forward and drove to a distance both her and the women and John.

Then Jesus cried out with a loud voice, saying: Father, let not this sin stand against them, for they know not what they do. Then he says: I thirst. And immediately there ran one of the soldiers and took a sponge and filled it with gall and vinegar mixed, and put it on a reed and gave to Jesus to drink. And, having tasted it, he would not drink it. And the Jews, standing and looking on, laughed at him, and said: If thou truly sayest that thou art the Son of God, come down from the cross immediately, that we may believe in thee.

Others said, mocking: Others he saved, others he cured, and he healed the sick, the paralytic, the lepers, the demoniacs, the blind, the lame, the dead; and himself he can not cure.

In the same manner, also, the robber crucified on his left hand said to him: If thou art the Son of God, come down and save both thyself and us. His name was Gistas. And he that was crucified on the right, Dysmas by name, reproved that robber, saying: O wretched and miserable man, dost thou not fear God? We suffer the due punishment of what we have done; but this man has done no evil at all. And, turning to Jesus, he says to him: Lord, when thou shalt reign, do not forget me. And he said to him: To-day, I tell thee truth, I shall have thee in paradise with me.

CHAP. 11.—Then Jesus, crying out with a loud voice, Father, into thy hands I shall commit my spirit, breathed his last. And immediately one could see the rocks rent; for there was an earthquake over all the earth; and from the earthquake being violent and great, the rocks also were rent. And the tombs of the dead were opened, and the curtain of the Temple was rent, and there was darkness from the sixth hour till the ninth. And from all these things that had happened the Jews were afraid, and said: Certainly this was a just man. And Longinus, the centurion who stood by, said: Truly this was the Son of God. Others coming and seeing him, beat their breasts from fear, and again turned back.

And the centurion, having perceived all these so great miracles, went away and reported them to Pilate. And when he heard he wondered and was astonished, and, from his fear and grief, would neither eat nor drink that day. And he sent notice, and all the Sanhedrim came to him as soon as the darkness was past; and he said to the people: You know how the sun has been darkened; you know how the curtain has been rent. Certainly I did well in being by no means willing to put to death the good man. And the malefactors said to Pilate: This darkness is an eclipse of the sun, such as has happened also at other times. Then they say to him: We hold the feast of unleavened bread to-morrow; and we entreat thee, since the crucified are still breathing, that their bones be broken, and that they be brought down. Pilate said: It shall be so. He therefore sent soldiers, and they found the two robbers yet breathing, and they broke their legs; but finding Jesus dead, they did not touch him at all, except that a soldier speared him in the right side, and immediately there came forth blood and water.

And as the [day of the] preparation was drawing towards evening, Joseph, a man well-born and rich, a God-fearing Jew, finding Nicodemus, whose sentiments his foregoing speech had shown, says to him: I know that thou didst love Jesus when living, and didst gladly hear his words, and I saw thee fighting with the Jews on his account. If, then, it seem good to thee, let us go to Pilate and beg the body of Jesus for burial, because it is a great sin for him to lie unburied. I am afraid, said Nicodemus, lest Pilate should be enraged, and some evil should befall me. But if thou wilt go alone and beg the dead and take him, then will I also go with thee and help thee do everything necessary for the burial. Nicodemus having thus spoken, Joseph directed his eyes to heaven and prayed that he might not fail in his request; and he went away to Pilate, and, having saluted him, sat down. Then he says to him: I entreat thee, my lord, not to be angry with me, if I shall ask anything contrary to what seems good to your highness. And he said: And what is it that thou askest? Joseph says: Jesus, the good man whom through hatred the Jews have taken away to crucify, him I entreat that thou give me for burial.

Pilate says: And what has happened that we should deliver to be honored again the dead body of him against whom evidence of sorcery was brought by his nation, and who was in suspicion of taking the kingdom of Cæsar, and so was given up by us to death? And Joseph, weeping and in great grief, fell at the feet of Pilate, saying: My lord, let no hatred fall upon a dead man; for all the evil that a man has done should perish with him in his death. And I know, your highness, how eager thou wast that Jesus should not be crucified, and how much thou saidst to the Jews on his behalf, now in entreaty and again in anger, and at last how thou didst wash thy hands and declare that thou wouldst by no means take part with those who wished him to be put to death; for all which [reasons] I entreat thee not to refuse my request. Pilate, therefore, seeing Joseph thus lying and supplicating and weeping, raised him up, and said: Go; I grant thee this dead man; take him and do whatever thou wilt.

And then Joseph, having thanked Pilate and kissed his hands and his garments, went forth, rejoicing indeed in heart as having obtained his desire, but carrying tears in his eyes. Thus, also, though grieved, he was glad. Accordingly, he goes away to Nicodemus and discloses to him all that had happened. Then, having bought myrrh and aloes a hundred pounds, and a new tomb, they, along with the mother of God and Mary Magdalene and Salome, along with John, and the rest of the women, did what was customary for the body with white linen, and placed it in the tomb.

And the mother of God said, weeping: How am I not to lament thee, my son? How should I not tear my face with my nails? This is that, my son, which Symeon the elder foretold to me when I brought thee, an infant of forty days old, into the Temple. This is the sword which now goes through my soul. Who shall put a stop to my tears, my sweetest son? No one at all except thyself alone, if, as thou saidst, thou shalt rise again in three days.

Mary Magdalene said, weeping: Hear, O peoples, tribes and tongues, and learn to what death the lawless Jews have delivered him who did them ten thousand good deeds. Hear and be astonished. Who will let these things be heard by all the world? I shall go alone to Rome to the Cæsar. I shall show him what evil Pilate hath done in obeying the lawless Jews. Likewise, also, Joseph lamented, saying: Ah, me! sweetest Jesus, most excellent of men, if, indeed, it be proper to

11

call thee man, who hast wrought such miracles as
no man has ever done. How shall I enshroud
thee? How shall I entomb thee? There should
now have been here those whom thou fedst with a
few loaves; for thus should I not have seemed to
fail in what is due.

Then Joseph, along with Nicodemus, went home;
and, likewise, also the mother of God, with the
women, John also being present with them.

CHAP. 12.—When the Jews were made acquainted
with these things done by Joseph and Nicodemus,
they were greatly stirred up against them. And
the chief priests Annas and Caiaphas sent for
Joseph, and said: Why hast thou done this service
to Jesus? Joseph says: I know that Jesus was a
man just and true and good in all respects; and I
know, also, that you, through hatred, managed to
murder him; and therefore I buried him. Then
the high priests were enraged, and laid hold of
Joseph and threw him into prison, and said to
him: If we had not to-morrow the feast of unleavened bread, to-morrow, also, should we have
put thee, like him, to death; but being kept in the
meantime, early in the morning of the Lord's day
thou shalt be given up to death. Thus they spoke,

and affixed their seal to the prison, having secured it by fastenings of all sorts.

Thus, therefore, when the preparation was ended, early on the Sabbath the Jews went away to Pilate, and said to him: My lord, that deceiver said that after three days he should rise again. Lest, therefore, his disciples should steal him by night and lead the people astray by such deceit, order his tomb to be guarded. Pilate therefore, upon this, gave them five hundred soldiers, who also, sat round the sepulchre so as to guard it, after having put seals upon the stone of the tomb.

The Lord's day, then, having dawned, the chief priests, along with the Jews, called a council and sent to take Joseph out of the prison, in order to put him to death. But, having opened it, they found him not. And they were astonished at this—how, with the doors shut and the bolts safe, and the seals unbroken, Joseph had disappeared.

CHAP. 13.—And upon this there came up one of the soldiers guarding the tomb, and he said in the synagogue: Learn that Jesus has risen. The Jews say: How? And he said: First there was an earthquake; then an angel of the Lord, clothed with lightning, came from heaven and rolled the stone from the tomb and sat upon it. And from fear of him all of us soldiers became as dead, and were able neither to flee nor speak. And we heard the angel saying to the women who came there to see the tomb: Be not you afraid, for I know that you seek Jesus. He is not here, but is risen, as he told you before. Bend down and see the tomb where his body lay; but go and tell his disciples that he is risen from the dead, and let them go into Galilee, for there shall they find him. For this reason I tell you this first.

The Jews say to the soldiers: What sort of women were they who came to the tomb? and why did you not lay hold of them? The soldiers say: From the fear and the mere sight of the angel, we were neither able to speak nor move. The Jews said: As the God of Israel liveth, we do not believe a word you say. The soldiers say: Jesus did so great wonders, and you believed not, and are you going to believe us? You say truly that God liveth; and certainly he whom you crucified truly liveth. But we have heard that you had Joseph shut up in the prison, and that you afterwards opened the doors and did not find him. Do you, then, present Joseph, and so we also shall present Jesus. The Jews say: Joseph, that fled from the prison, you will find in Arimathea, his own country. And the soldiers say: Go you into Galilee, and you will find Jesus, as the angel said to the woman.

At these [words] the Jews were afraid, and said to the soldiers: See that you tell this story to nobody, or all will believe in Jesus. And for this reason they gave them also much money. And the soldiers said: We are afraid lest by any chance Pilate hear that we have taken money, and he will kill us. And the Jews said: Take it; and we pledge ourselves that we shall speak to Pilate in your defense. Only say that you were asleep, and in your slumber the disciples of Jesus came and stole him from the tomb. The soldiers therefore took the money, and said as they were bid. And up to this day this same lying tale is told among the Jews.

CHAP. 14.—And a few days after there came from Galilee to Jerusalem three men. One of them was a priest, by name Phinees; the second a Levite, by name Aggai; and the third a soldier, by name Adas. These came to the chief priests, and said to them and to the people: Jesus, whom you crucified, we have seen in Galilee with his eleven disciples upon the Mount of Olives, teaching them, and saying, Go into all the world, and proclaim the good news; and whosoever will believe and be baptized shall be saved; but whosoever will not believe shall be condemned. And having thus spoken, he went up into heaven. And both we and many others of the five hundred besides were looking on.

And when the chief priests and the Jews heard these things, they said to these three: Give glory to the God of Israel, and repent of these lies that you have told. They answered: As the God of our fathers Abraham, Isaac, and Jacob liveth, we do not lie, but tell you the truth. Then the high priest spoke, and they brought the old [covenant] of the Hebrews out of the Temple, and he made them swear, and giving them also money, he sent them into another place, in order that they might not proclaim in Jerusalem the resurrection of Christ.

And when these stories had been heard by all the people, the crowd came together into the Temple, and there was a great commotion. For many said: Jesus has risen from the dead, as we hear, and why did you crucify him? And Annas and Caiaphas said: Do not believe, ye Jews, what the soldiers say; and do not believe that they saw an angel coming down from heaven. For we have given money to the soldiers, in order that they should not tell such tales to any one; and thus also have the disciples of Jesus given them money, in order that they should say that Jesus has risen from the dead.

CHAP. 15.—Nicodemus says: O children of the inhabitants of Jerusalem, the prophet Helias went up into the height of heaven with a fiery chariot, and it is nothing incredible if Jesus too has risen; for the prophet Helias was a prototype of Jesus, in order that you, hearing that Jesus has risen, might not disbelieve. I therefore say and advise, that it is befitting that we send soldiers into Galilee, to that place where these men testify that they saw him with his disciples, in order that they may go round about and find him, and that thus we may ask pardon of him for the evil which we have done to him. This proposal pleased them; and they chose soldiers, and sent them away into Galilee. And Jesus indeed they did not find; but they found Joseph in Arimathea.

When, therefore, the soldiers had returned, the chief priests, having ascertained that Joseph was found, brought the people together, and said: What shall we do to get Joseph to come to us? After deliberating, therefore, they wrote to him a letter to the following effect: O father Joseph, peace [be] to thee and all thy house, and thy friends! We know that we have offended against God, and

against thee his servant. On account of this, we
entreat thee to come here to us thy children. For
we have wondered much how thou didst escape
from the prison, and we say in truth that we had
an evil design against thee. But God, seeing that
our designs against thee were unjust, has delivered
thee out of our hands. But come to us, for thou
art the honor of our people.

This letter the Jews sent to Arimathea, with
seven soldiers, friends of Joseph. And they went
away and found him; and having respectfully
saluted him, as they had been ordered, they gave
him the letter. And after receiving it and reading
it, he glorified God, and embraced the soldiers; and
having set a table, ate and drank with them during
all the day and the night.

And on the following day he set out with them
to Jerusalem; and the people came forth to meet
him, and embraced him. And Nicodemus received
him into his own house. And the day after, Annas
and Caiaphas, the chief priests, having summoned
him to the Temple, said to him: Give glory to the
God of Israel, and tell us the truth. For we know
that thou didst bury Jesus; and on this account we
laid hold of thee, and locked thee up in the prison.
Thereafter, when we sought to bring thee out to be
put to death, we did not find thee, and we were

greatly astonished and afraid. Moreover, we prayed to God that we might find thee, and ask thee. Tell us therefore the truth.

Joseph said to them: In the evening of the preparation, when you secured me in prison, I fell a-praying throughout the whole night, and throughout the whole day of the Sabbath. And at midnight I see the prison-house that four angels lifted it up, holding it by the four corners. And Jesus came in like lightning, and I fell to the ground from fear. Taking hold of me, therefore, by the hand, he raised me, saying, Fear not, Joseph. Thereafter, embracing me, he kissed me, and said, Turn thyself, and see who I am. Turning myself, therefore, and looking, I said, My lord, I know not who thou art. He says, I am Jesus, whom thou didst bury the day before yesterday. I say to him, Show me the tomb, and then I shall believe. He took me, therefore, by the hand, and led me away to the tomb, which had been opened. And seeing the linen and the napkin, and recognizing him, I said, Blessed is he that cometh in the name of the Lord; and I adored him. Then taking me by the hand, and accompanied by the angels, he brought me to my house in Arimathea, and said to me, Sit here for forty days; for I go to my disciples, in order that I may enable them fully to proclaim my resurrection.

CHAP. 16.—When Joseph had thus spoken, the chief priests cried out to the people: We know that Jesus had a father and mother; how can we believe that he is the Christ? One of the Levites answered and said: I know the family of Jesus, noble-minded men, great servants of God, and receiving titles from the people of the Jews. And I know also Symeon the elder, that he received him when he was an infant, and said to him: Now thou sendest away thy servant, O Lord.

The Jews said: Let us now find the three men that saw him on the Mount of Olives, that we may question them, and learn the truth more accurately. They found them, and brought them before all, and made them swear to tell the truth. And they said: As the God of Israel liveth, we saw Jesus alive on the Mount of Olives, and going up into heaven.

Then Annas and Caiaphas took the three apart, one by one, and questioned them singly in private. They agreed with one another, therefore, and gave, even the three, one account. The chief priests answered, saying: Our Scripture says that every word shall be established by two or three witnesses. Joseph, then, has confessed that he, along with Nicodemus, attended to his body and buried him, and how it is the truth he has risen.

THE ACTS OF PILATE.

―――――

LATIN FORM.

I, Æneas, was at first a protector of the Hebrews,
and follower of the law; then the grace of the
Savior and his great gift took possession of me. I
recognized Christ Jesus in holy Scripture; I came
to him, and embraced his faith, so that I might
become worthy of his holy baptism. First of all I
searched for the memoirs written in those times
about our Lord Jesus Christ, which the Jews published in the age of Pontius Pilate, and we found
them in Hebrew writings, drawn up in the age of
the Lord Jesus Christ; and I translated them into
the language of the Gentiles, in the reign of the
eminent Theodosius, who was fulfilling his seventeenth consulship, and of Valentinian, consul for
the fifth time in the ninth indiction. Whosoever
of you read this book, and transfer it to other
copies, remember me, and pray for me, Æneas,
least of the servants of God, that he be merciful to

me, and pardon my sins which I have committed against him. Peace be to all who shall read these, and to all their house, for ever! Amen.

Now it came to pass, in the nineteenth year of the reign of Tiberius Cæsar, emperor of the Romans, and of Herod, son of Herod king of Galilee, in the nineteenth year of his rule, on the eighth day before the kalends of April, which is the twenty-fifth day of the month of March, in the consulship of Rufinus and Rubellio, in the fourth year of the 202d Olympiad, under the rule of Joseph and Caiaphas, priests of the Jews: the things done by the chief priests and the rest of the Jews, which Nicodemus recorded after the cross and passion of the Lord, Nicodemus himself committed to Hebrew letters.

CHAPTER. 1.—Annas and Caiaphas, Summas and Datam, Gamaliel, Judas, Levi, Neptalim, Alexander and Jairus, and the rest of the Jews, came to Pilate, accusing the Lord Jesus Christ of many things, and saying: We know him [to be] the son of Joseph the carpenter, born of Mary; and he says that he is the Son of God, and a king. Not only so, but he also breaks the Sabbath, and wishes to do away with the law of our fathers. Pilate says: What is it that he does, and wishes to destroy the law? The Jews say: We have a law, not to heal any one on the Sabbath; but he, by evil arts, heals on the Sabbath the lame and the hunchbacked, the blind, the palsied, the lepers, and the demoniacs. Pilate says to them: By what evil arts? They say to him: He is a sorcerer; and by Beelzebub, prince of the demons, he casts out demons, and they are all subject to him. Pilate says to them: It is not in an unclean spirit to cast out demons, but in the god of Scolapius.

The Jews say: We pray thy majesty to set him before thy tribunal to be heard. Pilate, calling the Jews to him, says to them: How can I, seeing that I am a governor, hear a king? They say to him: We do not say that he is a king, but he himself says he is. And Pilate, calling a runner, says to him: Let Jesus be brought in with kindness. And the runner, going out and recognizing him, adored him, and spread on the ground the cloak which he carried in his hand, saying: My lord, walk upon this, and come in, because the governor calls thee. But the Jews, seeing what the runner did, cried out against Pilate, saying: Why didst not thou make him come in by the voice of a crier, but by a runner? for the runner, too, seeing him, has adored him, and has spread out before him on the ground the cloak which he held in his hand, and has said to him: My lord, the governor calls thee.

And Pilate, calling the runner, says to him: Wherefore hast thou done this, and honored Jesus, who is called Christ? The runner says to him: When thou didst send me into Jerusalem to Alexander, I saw him sitting upon an ass, and the children of the Hebrews breaking branches from the trees, strewing them in the way; and others held branches in their hands; and others spread their garments in the way, shouting and saying, Save, therefore, thou who art in the highest; blessed [is he] that cometh in the name of the Lord!

The Jews cried out, saying against the runner: The children of the Hebrews indeed cried out in Hebrew. How canst thou, a Gentile, know this? The runner says to them: I asked one of the Jews, and said, What is it that they cry out in Hebrew? and he explained to me. Pilate says to them: And how did they cry out in Hebrew? The Jews said: Osanna in the highest! Pilate says to them: What is the meaning of Osanna in the highest? They say to him: Save us, thou who art in the highest. Pilate says to them: If you yourselves bear witness to these terms and words in which the children cried out, in what has the runner sinned? And they were silent. The governor says to the runner: Go out, and lead him in, in whatever way thou wilt. And the runner, going forth, did after the same form as before, and says to Jesus: My lord, go in, because the governor calls thee.

As Jesus, then, was going in, and the standard-bearers bearing the standards, the heads of the standards were bowed of themselves, and adored Jesus. And the Jews, seeing the standards, how they bowed themselves and adored Jesus, cried out the more against the standard-bearers. And Pilate says to the Jews: Do you not wonder at the way in which the standards have bowed themselves and adored Jesus? The Jews say to Pilate: We saw how the men carrying the standards bowed themselves and adored Jesus. And the governor, calling the standard-bearers, says to them: Why have you so done? They say to Pilate: We are Gentile men, and slaves of the temples: how had we to adore him? for when we were holding the figures, they themselves bowed and adored him.

Pilate says to the chiefs of the synagogue and the elders of the people: Choose ye men powerful and strong, and let them hold the standards, and let us see whether they will bow of themselves. And the elders of the Jews, taking twelve men very strong and powerful, made them hold the standards, six and six; and they stood before the governor's tribunal. Pilate says to the runner: Take out Jesus outside of the Pretorium, and bring

him in again, in whatever way thou wilt. And
Jesus and the runner went outside of the Pretorium. And Pilate, calling those who had formerly
held the standards, said to them: By the health of
Cæsar, if the standards do not bow themselves when
Jesus comes in, I will cut off your heads. And the
governor ordered Jesus to come in a second time.
And the runner did after the same form as before,
and besought Jesus much that he would go up and
walk upon his cloak. And he walked upon it, and
went in. And as Jesus was going in, immediately
the standards bowed themselves, and adored Jesus.

CHAP. 2.—And Pilate seeing, fear seized him, and
immediately he wished to rise from the tribunal.
And while he was thinking of this, [viz.] to rise
and go away, his wife sent to him, saying: Have
nothing to do with that just man, for I have suffered much on account of him this night. And
Pilate, calling the Jews, said to them: Ye know
that my wife is a worshiper of God, and in Juda-
ism thinks rather with you. The Jews say to him:
So it is, and we know. Pilate says to them: Lo,
my wife has sent to me, saying: Have nothing to
do with that just man, for I have suffered much on
account of him this night. And the Jews answering, said to Pilate: Did we not say to thee that he

is a magician? Lo, he has sent a vision of dreams to thy wife.

Pilate called Jesus, and said to him: What is it that these witness against thee, and sayst thou nothing to them? And Jesus answered: If they had not the power, they would not speak. Every one has power over his own mouth to say good and evil; let them see [to it].

And the elders of the Jews answering, say to Jesus: What shall we see? First, that thou wast born of fornication; second, that at thy birth in Bethlehem there took place a massacre of infants; third, that thy father Joseph and thy mother Mary fled into Egypt, because they had no confidence in the people.

Some of the bystanders, kind [men] of the Jews, say: We say that he was not born of fornication; but we know that Mary was espoused to Joseph, and that he was not born of fornication. Pilate says to the Jews who said that he was of fornication: This speech of yours is not true, seeing that the betrothal took place, as these of your nation say. Annas and Caiaphas say to Pilate: We, with all the multitude, say that he was born of fornication, and that he is a magician; but these are proselytes, and his disciples. And Pilate, calling

12

Annas and Caiaphas, says to them: What are proselytes? They say to him: They have been born sons of the Gentiles, and then have become Jews. Then answered those who testified that Jesus was not born of fornication, Lazarus and Asterius, Antonius and James, Annes and Azaras, Samuel and Isaac, Finees and Crispus, Agrippa and Judas: We were not born proselytes, but are sons of the Jews, and we speak the truth; for we were present at the betrothal of Mary.

And Pilate, calling to him those twelve men who proved that Jesus had not been born of fornication, said to them: I adjure you by the health of Cæsar, tell me if it be true that Jesus was not born of fornication. They say to Pilate: We have a law not to swear, because it is a sin; but let them swear by the health of Cæsar that it is not as we say, and we are worthy of death. Then said Pilate to Annas and Caiaphas: Answer you nothing to those things which these testify? Annas and Caiaphas say to Pilate: Those twelve are believed that he is not born of fornication; we—all the people—cry out that he was born of fornication, and is a magician, and says that he himself is the Son of God and a king, and we are not believed.

And Pilate ordered all the multitude to go outside, except the twelve men who said that he was

not born of fornication, and ordered to separate
Jesus from them. And Pilate says to them: For
what reason do the Jews wish to put Jesus to
death? And they say to him: They are angry
because he heals on the Sabbath. Pilate said: For
a good work do they wish to put him to death?
They say to him: Yes, my lord.

CHAP. 3.—Pilate, filled with fury, went forth outside of the Pretorium, and says to them: I take
the sun to witness that I find in this man not even
one fault. The Jews answered and said to the
governor: If he were not an evil-doer we should
never have delivered him to thee. Pilate says to
them: Take him and judge him according to your
law. The Jews answered: It is not permitted to
us to put any one to death. Pilate says to them:
Has God said to you not to put any one to death?
has he, therefore, said to me that I am to kill?

Pilate, having again gone into the Pretorium,
called Jesus to him privately, and said to him:
Art thou the king of the Jews? Jesus answered
Pilate: Speakest thou this of thyself, or have
others said [it] to thee of me? Pilate answered:
Am I a Jew? Thy nation and the chief priests
have delivered thee to me. What hast thou done?
Jesus, answering, said: My kingdom is not of this

world. If my kingdom were of this world, my servants would assuredly strive that I should not be delivered to the Jews; but now my kingdom is not from hence. Pilate said to him: Art thou then a king? Jesus said to him: Thou sayest that I am a king. For I for this was born, and for this have I come, that I should bear witness to the truth; and every one who is of the truth hears my voice. Pilate says to him: What is truth? Jesus says: Truth is from heaven. Pilate says: Is not there truth upon earth? Jesus says to Pilate: Notice how the truth-speaking are judged by those who have power upon earth.

CHAP. 4.—Pilate, therefore, leaving Jesus within the Pretorium, went out to the Jews, and says to them: I find not even one fault in him. The Jews say to him: He said, I can destroy that Temple, and in three days raise it again. Pilate said to them: What Temple? The Jews say to him: [The Temple] which Solomon built in forty and six years; and he says [that he can] destroy and build it in three days. Pilate says to them: I am innocent of the blood of this man; see ye [to it]. The Jews say to him: His blood [be] upon us and upon our children.

And Pilate, calling the elders and priests and

Levites, says to them privately: Do not do so; for in nothing, though you accuse him, do I find him deserving of death, not even about the healing and the breaking of the Sabbath. The priests and Levites and elders say: Tell us, if any one blasphemeth Cæsar, is he deserving of death or not? Pilate says to them: He deserves to die. The Jews answered him: How much more is he who has blasphemed God deserving to die!

And the governor ordered the Jews to go outside of the Pretorium; and, calling Jesus, said to him: What am to do with thee? Jesus says to Pilate: As it has been given [thee]. Pilate says: How has it been given? Jesus says: Moses and the prophets made proclamation of my death and resurrection. And the Jews, hearing this, say to Pilate: Why do you desire any more to hear blasphemy? And Pilate said: If this speech is blasphemous, do you take him and lead him to your synagogue and judge him according to your law. The Jews say to Pilate: Our law holds, If a man have sinned against a man, he is worthy to receive forty less one; but he who has blasphemed against God, to be stoned.

Pilate says to them: Then judge him according to your law. The Jews say to Pilate: We wish that he be crucified.   Pilate says to them : He does not deserve to be crucified.

And the governor, looking upon the people of the Jews standing round, saw very many of the Jews weeping, and said : All the multitude does not wish him to die.   The elders say to Pilate : And for this reason have we come—the whole multitude—that he should die.   Pilate said to the Jews : What has he done that he should die ?   They say : Because he said that he was the Son of God, and a king.

CHAP. 5.—But one Nicodemus, a Jew, stood before the governor, and said : I entreat mercifully, allow me to say a few words.   Pilate says to him : Say on.   Nicodemus says : I said to the elders and the priests and the Levites, and to all the multitude of the Jews in the synagogue, What have you [to do] with this man ?   This man does many wonders and signs, which no one of men has done or can do.   Let him go, and do not devise any evil against him ; if the signs which he does are of God, they will stand ; but if of men, they will come to nothing.   For Moses, also, being sent by God into Egypt, did many signs, which God told him to do before Pharaoh, king of Egypt.   And the sorcerers, Jamnes and Mambres, were there healing, and they

did, they also, the signs which Moses did, but not
all; and the Egyptians deemed them as gods, Jamnes
and Mambres. And since the signs which they
did were not of God, they perished, both they and
those who believed in them. And now let this
man go, for he is not deserving of death.

The Jews say to Nicodemus: Thou hast become
his disciple, and takest his part. Nicodemus says
to them: Has the governor also become his disciple, and does he take his part? Has not Cæsár
set him over that dignity? And the Jews were
raging and gnashing with their teeth against Nicodemus. Pilate says to them: Why do you gnash
with your teeth against him, [when you are] hearing the truth? The Jews say to Nicodemus:
Mayst thou receive his truth, and a portion with
him! Nicodemus says: Amen, amen, amen; may
I receive [it], as you have said!

CHAP. 6.—And of the Jews a certain other one,
starting up, asks the governor that he might say a
word. The governor says: What thou wishest to
say, say. And he said: For thirty-eight years I
lay in infirmity in my bed in very grievous pain.
And at the coming of Jesus many demoniacs, and
[persons] held down by divers infirmities, were
healed by him. And some young men had pity on

me, and, carrying me in my bed, laid me before him. And Jesus, seeing, had pity on me, and said the word to me, Take up thy bed and walk. And immediately l was made whole; I took up my bed and walked. The Jews say to Pilate: Ask him what was the day on which he was healed. He said: The Sabbath. The Jews say: Have we not so informed thee, that on the Sabbath he heals and drives out demons?

.And a certain other Jew, starting up, said: I was born blind; I heard a voice and saw no man. And as Jesus was passing by I cried out with a loud voice, Have pity upon me, thou son of David. And he had pity upon me, and laid his hands upon my eyes, and I saw immediately. And another Jew, starting up, said: I was hunchbacked, and he straightened me with a word. And another said: I was leprous, and he healed me with a word.

CHAP. 7.—And also a certain woman, Veronica by name, from afar off cried out to the governor: I was flowing with blood for twelve years; and I touched the fringe of his garment, and immediately the flowing of my blood stopped. The Jews say: We have a law that a woman does not come to bear witness.

CHAP. 8.—And certain others, a multitude of

men and women, cried out, saying: That man is a prophet, and the demons are subject to him. Pilate says to those who said the demons are subject to him: And your masters, why are they not subject to him? They say to Pilate: We do not know. And others said to Pilate: He raised up dead Lazarus from the tomb after four days. The governor, hearing this, said trembling to all the multitude of the Jews: Why do you wish to shed innocent blood?

CHAP. 9.—And Pilate, calling Nicodemus and the twelve men who said that he was not born of fornication, says to them: What am I to do, seeing that there is a sedition among the people? They say to him: We do not know; let them see to it. Again Pilate, calling all the multitude of the Jews, said: You know that you have a custom during the day of unleavened bread, that I should release to you one that is bound. I have a notable one bound in the prison, a murderer who is called Barabbas, and Jesus who is called Christ, in whom I find no cause of death. Whom do you wish that I should release unto you? And they all cried out, saying: Release unto us Barabbas. Pilate says to them: What, then, am I to do with Jesus who is called Christ? They all say: Let him be crucified. Again the Jews said: Thou art no friend of Cæsar's if thou release this man, for he called himself the Son of God, and a king; unless, perhaps, thou wishest this man to be king, and not Cæsar.

Then, filled with fury, Pilate said to them: Always has your nation been seditious, and always have you been opposed to those who were for you. The Jews answered: Who are for us? Pilate says to them: Your God, who rescued you from the hard slavery of the Egyptians, and led you forth out of Egypt through the sea as if through dry land, and fed you in the desert with manna and quail, and brought water to you out of the rock and gave you to drink, and gave you a law; and in all these things you provoked your God, and sought for yourselves a god—a molten calf. And you exasperated your God, and he wished to slay you; and Moses made supplication for you, that ye should not die. And now you say that I hate the king.

And, rising up from the tribunal, he wished to go outside. And the Jews cried out and said to him: We know that Cæsar is king, and not Jesus. For the magi also presented gifts to him as a king; and Herod, hearing from the magi that a king was born, wished to slay him. But when this was known, his father, Joseph, took him and his mother and fled into Egypt; and Herod, hearing, destroyed the infants of the Jews which were born in Bethlehem.

Pilate, hearing these words, was afraid. And, silence being made among the people who were crying out, Pilate said: This, then, is he whom Herod sought? They say to him: It is he. And, taking water, Pilate washed his hands in presence of the people, saying: I am innocent of the blood of this just man; see ye to it. Again the Jews cried out, saying: His blood [be] upon us and upon our children.

Then Pilate ordered the veil to be loosened, and said to Jesus: Thine own nation have brought charges against thee as a king; and, therefore, I have sentenced thee first to be scourged on account of the statutes of the emperors, and then to be crucified on the cross.

CHAP. 10.—And when Jesus was scourged, he delivered him to the Jews to be crucified, and two robbers with him; one by name Dismas, and the other by name Gestas. And when they came to the place, they stripped him of his garments and girt him about with a linen cloth, and put a crown of thorns upon his head. Likewise, also, they hanged the two robbers with him, Dismas on the right and Gestas on the left. And Jesus said: Father, forgive them, for they know not what they do. And the soldiers parted his garments among them. And the people stood waiting; and their chief priests and judges mocked him, saying among themselves: He saved others, now let him save himself; if he is the Son of God, 'let him come down from the cross. And the soldiers mocked him, falling prostrate before him, and offering him vinegar with gall, and saying: If thou art the king of the Jews, set thyself free.

And Pilate, after sentence, orderad a title to be written in Hebrew, Greek and Latin letters, according to what the Jews said: This is the King of the Jews.

And one of the robbers [who were] hanged, by name Gestas, said to him: If thou art the Christ, free thyself and us. And Dismas, answering, rebuked him, saying: Dost not even thou fear God, who art in condemnation? for we justly and deservedly have received those things which we endure; but he has done no evil. And he kept saying to Jesus: Remember me, Lord, in thy kingdom. And Jesus said to him: Verily I say unto thee, that to-day shalt thou be with me in paradise.

CHAP. 11.—And it was about the sixth hour, and there was darkness over the whole earth; and the sun was obscured, and the veil of the Temple was rent in the midst. And, crying out with a loud voice, he said: Father, into thy hands I commend my spirit. And thus saying, he gave up the ghost. And the centurion, seeing what was done, glorified God, saying: This was a just man. And all the people who were present at that spectacle, seeing what was done, beating their breasts, returned.

And the centurion reported to the governor what was done. And the governor and his wife hearing, were very sorrowful, and neither ate nor drank that day. And Pilate, calling together the Jews, said to them: Have you seen what has been done? And they said to the governor: There has been an eclipse of the sun, as is usual.

And his acquaintances stood afar off, and the women who had followed him from Galilee, seeing these things. And lo, a certain man, by name Joseph, holding office—a man good and just, who did not consent to their counsels nor their deeds, from Arimathea, a city of the Jews, waiting—he, also, for the kingdom of God, went to Pilate and begged the body of Jesus. And, taking him down from the cross, he wrapped him in clean linen and laid him in his own new tomb, in which no one had been laid.

CHAP. 12.—And the Jews, hearing that Joseph had begged the body of Jesus, sought for him; and those twelve men who had said that he was not born of fornication, and Nicodemus and many others who had stood before Pilate and declared his good works. And all of them being hid, Nicodemus alone appeared to them, because he was a chief man of the Jews; and he says to them: How have ye come into the synagogue? The Jews say to him: And thou, how hast thou come into the synagogue, seeing that thou consentest with him? May his portion be with thee in the world to come! Nicodemus said: Amen, amen, amen. Likewise also Joseph, coming forth, said to them: Why are you enraged against me because I begged the body of Jesus? Lo, I have laid him in my own new tomb, wrapping him in clean linen; and I have rolled a stone to the door of the cave. And ye have not acted well against a just man, since you have not borne in mind how you crucified him and pierced him with a lance. The Jews, therefore, laying hold of Joseph, ordered him to be imprisoned because of the Sabbath day; and they say to him: Know that the hour compels us not to do anything against thee, because the Sabbath is dawning. But understand that thou art worthy not even of burial, but we will give thy flesh to the birds of the air and the beasts of the earth. Joseph says to them: That is the speech of the proud Goliath, who reviled the living God against holy David. And God hath said, Vengeance is mine; I will repay, saith the Lord. And Pilate, intercepted in his heart, took water, and washed his hands before the sun, saying, I am innocent of the blood of this just man; see ye to it. And you answered and said to Pilate, His blood be upon us, and upon our children. And now I fear that some time or other the wrath of God will come upon you and your children, as you have said. And the Jews, hearing this, were embittered in heart; and taking Joseph, shut him up in a house where there was no window, and set guards at the gates, and sealed the gate where Joseph had been shut up.

And on the Sabbath morning they took counsel with the priests and the Levites, that they should all be assembled after the Sabbath day. And awaking at dawn, all the multitude in the synagogue took counsel by what death they should slay him. And when the assembly was sitting, they ordered him to be brought with much indignity; and opening the gate, they found him not. All the people therefore were in terror, and wondered with exceeding astonishment, because they found the seals sealed, and because Caiaphas had the keys. And no longer did they dare to lay hand upon those who spoke before Pilate in Jesus' defense.

CHAP. 13.—And while they were sitting in the synagogue, and recriminating about Joseph, there came certain of the guards whom they had asked from Pilate to guard the sepulchre of Jesus, lest his disciples coming should steal him. And they reported, saying to the rulers of the synagogue, and the priests and the Levites, what had happened: how there had happened a great earthquake, and we saw how an angel of the Lord came down from heaven, and rolled away the stone from the door of the tomb, and sat upon it; and his countenance was like lightning, and his raiment like snow. And for fear, we became as dead. And we heard the voice of the angel speaking to the women who had come to the sepulchre, and saying, Be not ye afraid; for I know that ye seek Jesus who was crucified: He is not here; he has risen, as he said: come and see the place where the Lord was laid. And go immediately and tell his disciples that he has risen from the dead, and will go before you into Galilee, as he said to you.

The Jews say: To what women was he speaking?

The soldiers say: We do not know who the women were. The Jews say: At what hour was it? The guards say: At midnight. The Jews say: And why did you not detain them? The guards say: We became as dead from fear of the angel, not hoping now to see the light of day; and how could we detain them? The Jews say: [As] the Lord God liveth, we do not believe you. And the guards said to the Jews: You have seen so great signs in that man, and have not believed; and how can you believe us, that the Lord lives? For well have ye sworn that the Lord Jesus Christ lives. Again the guards say to the Jews: We have heard that you have shut up Joseph, who begged the body of Jesus, in the prison, and have sealed it with your rings; and on opening, that you have not found him. Give us Joseph, then, and we shall give you Jesus Christ. The Jews said: Joseph has gone to Arimathea, his own city. The guards say to the Jews: And Jesus, as we have heard from the angel, is in Galilee.

And the Jews, hearing these sayings, feared exceedingly, saying: Lest at some time or other this saying be heard, and all believe in Jesus. And the Jews, taking counsel among themselves, brought forth a sufficient number of silver pieces, and gave

13

to the soldiers, saying: Say that, while we slept, his disciples came and stole him. And if this be heard by the governor, we shall persuade him, and make you secure. And the soldiers, taking [the money], said as they were advised by the Jews, and their saying was spread abroad among all.

CHAP. 14.—And Finees a certain priest, and Addas a teacher, and Egias a Levite, coming down from Galilee to Jerusalem, reported to the rulers of the synagogue, and the priests and the Levites, how they had seen Jesus sitting, and his disciples with him, on the Mount of Olivet, which is called Mambre, or Malech. And he said to his disciples: Go into all the world, and declare to every creature the gospel of the kingdom of God. He who believeth and is baptized shall be saved; but he who believeth not shall be condemned. And these signs shall follow them who believe: In my name shall they cast out demons; they shall speak in new tongues; they shall take up serpents; and if they have drunk any deadly thing, it shall not hurt them; they shall lay hands upon the sick, and they shall be well. And as Jesus was thus speaking to his disciples, we saw him taken up into heaven.

The priests and the Levites and the elders say to them: Give glory to the God of Israel, and give

confession to him, whether you have both heard
and seen those things which you have related.
Those who had made the report say: As the Lord
God of our fathers liveth, the God of Abraham,
and the God of Isaac, and the God of Jacob, we
have heard and seen. The Jews say to them: Have
you come for this—to tell us? or have you come
to give prayer to God? They said: We have come
to give prayer to God. The elders and chief priests
and Levites say to them: And if you have come
to give prayer to God, why have you murmured
before all the people about that foolish tale? Finees
the priest, and Addas the teacher, and Egias the
Levite, say to the rulers of the synagogue, and the
priests and the Levites: If those words which we
have spoken, which we have seen and heard, be
sin, behold, we are in your presence; do unto us
according to that which is good in your eyes. And
they, taking the law, adjured them to report the
words to no one thereafter. And they gave them
to eat and drink, and put them outside of the city,
giving them silver pieces, and three men with them,
who should conduct them as far as Galilee.

Then the Jews took counsel among themselves
when those men had gone up into Galilee; and
the rulers of the synagogue shut themselves in, and
were cut up with great fury, saying: What sign is

this which hath come to pass in Israel? And Annas and Caiaphas say: Why are your souls sorrowful? Are we to believe the soldiers, that an angel of the Lord came down from heaven, and rolled away the stone from the door of the tomb? [No]; but that his disciples have given much gold to those who were guarding the sepulchre, and have taken Jesus away, and have taught them thus to say: Say ye that an angel of the Lord came down from heaven, and rolled away the stone from the door of the tomb. Do you not know that it is unlawful for Jews to believe foreigners in a single word, knowing that these same who received sufficient gold from us have said as we taught them?

CHAP. 15.—And Nïcodemus rising up, stood in the midst of the council, and said: You have said rightly. And are not the men who have come down from Galilee God-fearing, men of peace, hating a lie? And they recounted with an oath, how "we saw Jesus sitting on Mount Mambre with his disciples, and he taught them in our hearing," and that they saw him taken up into heaven. And no one asked them this: How he was taken up into heaven. And, as the writing of the holy book teaches us, holy Elias too was taken up into heaven, and Elisæus cried out with a loud voice, and Elias

threw his sheepskin over Elisæus; and again Elisæus threw that sheepskin over the Jordan, and
went over and came to Jericho. And the sons of
the prophets met him, and said to Elisæus, Where
is thy master Elias? And he said, He has been
taken up into heaven. And they said to Elisæus,
Has a spirit snatched him away, and thrown him
upon one of the mountains? But rather let us
take our boys with us and seek him. And they
persuaded Elisæus, and he went with them. And
they sought him for three days and three nights,
and found him not, because he was taken up. And
now, men, hear me, and let us send into all Israel,
and see lest Jesus can have been taken up some-
where or other, and thrown upon one of the mountains. And that saying pleased all. And they
sent to all the mountains of Israel to seek Jesus,
and they found him not; but they found Joseph
of Arimathea, and no one dared to lay hold of him.

And they reported to the elders and priests and
Levites: We have gone round all the mountains
of Israel, and not found Jesus; but we have found
Joseph in Arimathea. And hearing of Joseph,
they rejoiced, and gave glory to the God of Israel.
And the rulers of the synagogue, and the priests
and the Levites, taking counsel in what manner

they should send to Joseph, took paper, and wrote
to Joseph:

Peace to thee and all that is thine! We know
that we have sinned against God, and against thee;
and thou hast prayed to the God of Israel, and he
has delivered thee out of our hands. And now
deign to come to thy fathers and thy children, because we have been vehemently grieved. We have
all sought for thee—we who opened the door, and
found thee not. We know that we counseled evil
counsel against thee; but the Lord hath supplanted
our counsel against thee. Thou art worthy to be
honored, father Joseph, by all the people.

And they chose out of all Israel seven men
friendly to Joseph, whom also Joseph knew to be
friendly; and the rulers of the synagogue and the
priests and the Levites say to them: See, if he take
the letter and read it, for certain he will come with
you to us; but if he do not read it, you may know
that he is ill-disposed toward us, and, saluting him
in peace, return to us. And blessing them, they
sent them away. And they came to Arimathea to
Joseph, and adored him on their face upon the
ground, and said: Peace to thee and all thine!
And Joseph said: Peace to you, and to all the people of Israel! And they gave him the roll of the
letter. And Joseph took and read it, and rolled up

the letter, and blessed God, and said: Blessed [be]
the Lord God, who hath delivered Israel from shed-
ding innocent blood; and blessed [be] God, who
sent his angel, and covered me under his wings.
And he kissed them, and set a table for them; and
they ate and drank, and slept there.

And they rose in the morning; and Joseph saddled his ass, and traveled with them, and they came
into the holy city Jerusalem. And there met them
all the people, crying out, and saying: Peace [be]
in thy coming in, father Joseph! To whom he
answered and said: The peace of the Lord [be]
upon all the people! And they all kissed him.
And they prayed with Joseph, and were terrified
at the sight of him. And Nicodemus took him
into his house, and made a great feast, and called
Annas and Caiaphas, and the elders and chief
priests and Levites, to his house. And making
merry, and eating and drinking with Joseph, they
blessed God, and went every one to his own house.
And Joseph remained in the house of Nicodemus.

And on the next day, which is the preparation,
the priests and the rulers of the synagogue and the
Levites rose early, and came to the house of Nicodemus. And Nicodemus met them, and said to
them: Peace to you! And they said to him: Peace
to thee and Joseph, and to thy house and Joseph's

house! And Nicodemus brought them into his house. And the counsel sat; and Joseph sat between Annas and Caiaphas, and no one dared to say a word. And Joseph said to them: Why have you called me? And they made signs with their eyes to Nicodemus, that he should speak with Joseph. And Nicodemus opening his mouth, said: Father Joseph, thou knowest that the reverend teachers, priests, and Levites seek to hear a word from thee. And Joseph said: Ask. And Annas and Caiaphas, taking up the law, adjured Joseph, saying: Give glory to the God of Israel, and give confession to him, that thou wilt not hide any word from us. And they said to him: With grief were we grieved that thou didst beg the body of Jesus, and wrap it in clean linen, and lay it in a tomb. Therefore we shut thee up in a house where there was no window, and put a lock and a seal on the gate; and on the first day of the week we opened the gates, and found thee not. We were therefore exceedingly grieved, and astonishment came over all the people of God. And therefore hast thou been sent for; and now tell us what has happened.

Then said Joseph: On the day of the preparation, about the tenth hour, you shut me in, and I remained there the whole Sabbath in full. And when midnight came, as I was standing and pray-

ing, the house where you shut me in was hung up
by the four corners, and there was a flashing of light
in mine eyes. And I fell to the ground trembling.
Then some one lifted me up from the place where
I had fallen, and poured over me an abundance of
water from the head even to the feet, and put round
my nostrils the odor of a wonderful ointment, and
rubbed my face with the water itself, as if washing
me, and kissed me, and said to me, Joseph, fear
not; but open thine eyes, and see who it is that
speaks to thee. And looking, I saw Jesus; and
being terrified, I thought it was a phantom. And
with prayer and the commandments I spoke to him,
and he spoke with me. And I said to him: Art
thou Rabbi Elias? And he said to me: I am not
Elias. And I said: Who art thou, my lord? And
he said to me: I am Jesus, whose body thou didst
beg from Pilate, and wrap in clean linen; and thou
didst lay a napkin on my face, and didst lay me in
thy new tomb, and roll a stone to the door of the
tomb. Then I said to him that was speaking to
me: Show me, Lord, where I laid thee. And he
led me, and showed me the place where I laid him,
and the linen which I had put on him, and the
napkin which I had wrapped upon his face; and I
knew that it was Jesus. And he took hold of me
with his hand, and put me in the midst of my house

though the gates were shut, and put me in my bed, and said to me: Peace to thee! And he kissed me, and said to me: For forty days go not out of thy house; for, lo, I go to my brethren into Galilee.

CHAP. 16.—And the rulers of the synagogue, and the priests and the Levites, hearing these words from Joseph, became as it were dead, and fell to the ground, and fasted until the ninth hour. And Joseph and Nicodemus entreated them, saying: Arise and stand upon your feet, and taste bread, and comfort your souls, seeing that to-morrow is the Sabbath of the Lord. And they arose, and entreated the Lord, and ate and drank, and went every man to his own house.

And on the Sabbath the teachers and doctors sat questioning each other, and saying: What is this wrath that has come upon us? because we know his father and mother. Levi the teacher said: I know that his parents fear God, and never depart from prayer, and give tithes thrice a year. And when Jesus was born, his parents brought him up to this place, and gave to God sacrifices and burnt offerings. And assuredly the great teacher Simeon took him into his arms, saying: Now thou sendest away thy servant, O Lord, according to thy word, in peace; for mine eyes have seen thy salvation, which thou hast prepared before the face of all peoples, a light for the revealing of the nations, and the glory of thy people Israel. And he blessed Mary his mother, and said, I make an announcement to thee concerning this child. And Mary said, Well, my lord. And Simeon said, Well. And he said again, Lo, he has been set for the fall and rising again of many in Israel, and for a sign which shall be spoken against; and a sword shall pierce thine own soul, that the thoughts of many hearts may be revealed.

And the Jews said to Levi: And how knowest thou these things? Levi says: Do you not know that from him I learned the law? They of the council say: We wish to see thy father. And they searched out his father, and got information; for he said: Why did you not believe my son? The ·blessed and just Simeon taught him the law. The council says to Rabbi Levi: The saying which thou hast spoken is true. The chief priests and rulers of the synagogue, and Levites, said to each other: Come, let us send into Galilee to the three men who came hither and gave an account of his teaching and his being taken up, and let them tell us how they saw him taken up into heaven. And that saying pleased all. Then they sent three men into Galilee; and Go, said they, say to Rabbi Addas and

Rabbi Finees and Rabbi Egias, Peace to you and yours! Many investigations have been made in the council concerning Jesus; therefore have we been instructed to call you to the holy place, to Jerusalem.

The men went to Galilee, and found them sitting, and meditating on the law. And they saluted them in peace. And they said: Why have you come? The messengers said: The council summon you to the holy city Jerusalem. And the men, hearing that they were sought for by the council, prayed to God, and reclined with the men, and ate and drank with them. And rising in the morning, they went to Jerusalem in peace.

And on the morrow the council sat; and they questioned them, saying: Did you plainly see Jesus sitting on Mount Mambre teaching his disciples, and taken up into heaven?

First Addas the teacher says: I really saw him sitting on Mount Mambre teaching his disciples; and a shining cloud overshadowed him and his disciples, and he went up into heaven; and his disciples prayed upon their faces on the ground. And calling Finees the priest, they questioned him also, saying: How didst thou see Jesus taken up? And he said the same as the other. And again they called the third, Rabbi Egias, and questioned him,

and he said the same as the first and second. And
those who were in the council said: The law of
Moses. holds that by the mouth of two or three
every word should stand. Abudem, a teacher, one
of the doctors, says: It is written in the law, Enoch
walked with God, and was translated; for God
took him. Jairus, a teacher, said: And we have
heard of the death of holy Moses, and have not
seen [it]; for it is written in the law of the Lord,
And Moses died according to the word of the Lord,
and no man knoweth of his burying even to the
present day. Rabbi Levi said: What is it that
Rabbi Simeon said? Lo, he lies for the fall and
rising again of many in Israel, and for a sign
which shall be spoken against? Rabbi Isaac said:
It is written in the law, Lo, I send mine angel,
who shall go before thy face to keep thee in every
good way, because I have brought his new name.

Then Annas and Caiaphas said: Rightly have ye
said that these things are written in the law of
Moses that no one saw the death of Enoch, and no
one has named the burying of holy Moses. And
Jesus gave account to Pilate, and we saw him
scourged and receiving spitting on his face; and
the soldiers put a crown of thorns on him, and he
received sentence from Pilate; and then he was
crucified, and they gave him gall and vinegar to

drink; and two robbers were crucified with him, and the soldier Longinus pierced his side with a lance; and our honorable father Joseph begged his body, and he has risen again, and, as they say, the three teachers have seen him taken up into heaven. And Rabbi Levi has borne witness to what was said by Simeon the elder—that he has been set for the fall and rising again of many in Israel, and for a sign which shall be spoken against.

Then Didas, a teacher, said to all the assembly: If all the things which these have borne witness to have come to pass in Jesus, they are from God, and let it not be wonderful in our eyes. The chiefs of the synagogue, and the priests and the Levites said to each other how our law holds, saying: His name shall be blessed forever: His place endureth before the sun, and his seat before the moon; and all the tribes of earth shall be blessed in him, and all nations shall serve him; and kings shall come from far, adoring and magnifying him.

Ingram Content Group UK Ltd.
Milton Keynes UK
UKHW020607250423
420723UK00005B/86